Dear Katie

thank you for laughing with us
the Tuscan way!

THE TUSCAN WHO
SOLD HIS FIAT
TO THE POPE

The Tuscan Who Sold His Fiat to the Pope

Stories from Tuscany to California about Family, Food, Religion, Sex, and the Art of Laughing the Italian Way

Samuele Bagnai

Printed in the United States of America

First Printing, 2019

ISBN-10: 1-942489-71-4
ISBN-13: 978-1-942489-71-9

For my Grandma

How beautiful our Youth is
That's always flying by us!
Who'd be happy, let him be so:
Nothing's sure about tomorrow.
            —Lorenzo de' Medici

The white page stares at me
Will I dare to write on it?
Let the ink follow my heart
And the words one another
Without judging what I think
Instead, enjoying the moment
Of making ideas into forms
A reflection of myself
And the world as I see it?

I am immersed in the silence
That implores me to keep going
To say what's in my mind
Not to have shame of it
Neither for its simplicity
Neither for being unique
This pure song that comes from within
I would like to share it with you
My friend, far away and close to me.
— Samuele Bagnai

TABLE OF CONTENTS

Part I The Stories

Part II Carnival of Poems

PART I

THE STORIES

When You're Here, You're Family

A *casa mia* (at my home) is an arrogant declaration used by Tuscan people, implying that "at my house" we think, do, and behave in a certain way, which obviously is better than what goes on at your house. "At my house, we use béchamel rather than ricotta to make lasagna," said my grandmother, who was unwilling to compromise in her kitchen.

The concepts of home, family, and tradition are essential to Italian culture. Any Italian will tell you that family trumps all. It's no wonder, then, that the Olive Garden restaurant chose the tagline "When you're here, you're family." The slogan is vague and obviously a marketing tool; however, it proves that the concept of family has the potential to increase revenue, basically because people have a need to belong, and they value simple things such as sharing a meal at a table with Grandma and Grandpa. But I hope people realize that the Olive Garden isn't going to give you what they're advertising. Family has no monetary value. Family is family. The most that you can get out of the Olive Garden is eating some mix-and-match cuisine, a blend of pasta and pico de gallo, or chicken Alfredo (which doesn't exist in Italy).

To better understand the Italian concept of family, I will illustrate the story of an American friend of mine who went to Naples on a vacation alongside his fiancée and another couple. During their trip, they stopped at a restaurant on the bay. They ordered dinner and were very satisfied with the quality and service. They paid their bill, which was $200 (US), which seemed reasonable based on what they ate. In fact, they decided to go back the next night. They consumed the same food, and when the bill came, they were surprised to find out that it was only $100. There had to be a mistake. Personally, I would have paid and moved on, but my curious friend couldn't help but inquire about the discrepancy. Was Tuesday night special? Maybe there were happy-hour prices? My friend went to the hostess, who was the owner of the restaurant, and pointed out the mistake. The owner told him that there was no mistake, adding in a friendly voice, "You see, last night you were a tourist. Tonight, you are family!"

When it comes to Italian hospitality, my family is no exception. Every month, my father organized a dinner at our home. My mother was never given much time to prepare for these occasions, even though most of the work was her responsibility. Those dinners were significant to my family, as we entertained people from church, work, and our neighborhood.

The dining room at our home had a long mahogany table that could seat at least forty people. The dishes, bowls, and pitchers were hand painted by a local artist, Arnaldo Miniati, who was well known for his realistic imagery of the beautiful landscapes of Tuscany.

As a child, I always worried that my dad would spend all our money on these dinners and we'd become homeless. One night, I prepared a sign, which I placed next to a bowl at the door. It said: "If you came here for cocktails, the price is fifty cents; the price for the all-inclusive dinner is one dollar." One guest, the local priest, called me into the living room where he was sitting with my dad and some of the other guests. He said, "I saw the sign at the door, and I completely agree. Here is my share." And with a smile, he handed me a dollar. He was the only one to give me money, but everyone thought that my anxiety was cute. I must have had a premonition, because my dad did in fact lose all his money. This had to do with globalization and competition from developing countries. My father's textile industry could not adapt to the lower costs of production, primarily because these countries were willing to work harder for less money. However, my theory was that these workers had heard of the glorious dinners of lasagna, linguine, and mortadella that my dad hosted, and were inspired to live that kind of life at any cost.

On this particular night, the guests slowly filed into the dining room. Then, when everybody was seated, my father signaled a moment of silence to thank God for this gathering, for the food, and for all of our many blessings. Following the "Amen," the Tuscan appetizer was rolled out onto the table, the Chianti was poured into everyone's glasses, and my father said a toast for health and prosperity.

The window overlooking the street offered a glimpse outside. The rhythmic, summery tunes of the crickets played unabatingly. Inside, the golden, elegant chandelier reflected the light with its crystals, much like an engraved crown rising to illuminate the big table.

Between the hall and the kitchen, there was a great bustle of courses moving in and out. Every detail of every dish had been carefully prepared by my mother, with the help of my aunt and grandma. Panzanella, a popular summer dish, was served first, along with beef carpaccio. The alternative for those with sensitive stomachs was tortellini served in chicken broth. The main dish was roast chicken and polenta. For dessert, the guests were served apple cake paired with a shot of grappa, of the finest quality and highest alcohol content, to aid in digestion.

It was almost eleven o' clock, but I didn't want to go to sleep. It was amazing to hear all the conversations and laughter in this atmosphere of true joviality. Eventually, the guests went home. My siblings and I helped clear the table and sweep the floor.

Even though my mother would grumble when the next invitations were sent out a month later, she was probably the happiest of all to open her home to the same folks. What could have been better than spending time together and indulging in the pleasures of life? Epicurus once said that life is made to celebrate, have a good time, and thank the Almighty for the precious moments shared with one another. This is the feeling of family that the Olive Garden can only dream of delivering. Dinners at my house were *truly* a "When you're here, you're family" type of event.

Variety is what makes the world beautiful. In Italy, the dissimilarities between the northern and southern regions are reflected in everyday life and in family as well. In the north, people are more individualistic than in the south, which values the group dynamic. Therefore, as you travel south, the stereotype of the Italian-family idea becomes more evident given the overwhelming warmth and affection. Tuscany is right in the middle of the two extremes: we are warmer than the Milanese people but not as warm as the Sicilians. I was able to experience the southern type of family when I visited my friend Beppe in Bari, who lived at the southern tip of the Italian boot.

I got a call from Beppe in early December one year. He wanted me to visit for New Year's Eve. It was my first time visiting a city south of Rome. I was going to travel at night, and it would take about ten hours to get directly to Bari. I got on the train a couple of days after Christmas. That was the cheapest way to travel, as I couldn't afford to fly. Also, traveling in this way would add some adventure to my journey because I knew I was going to meet all kinds of people on the train. I wasn't disappointed.

The trains that go to Southern Italy have a distinctive smell of food, and they move slower because of the tons of products that passengers carry with them. If Italian people love food, in the south, it's double the love. As the train left the station in Florence, I could smell the cheese and the salami, and hear people laughing and pouring wine. I think that this train is the only one where the passengers sell food to the restaurant on board when it's short on items, instead of the other way around.

I got off the train in Bari, and Beppe and his girlfriend came to greet me. When we got to his grandparents' house, it was still early in the morning. There was an abundance of kisses and hugs from both familiar and unfamiliar faces. After I'd settled into the guest room, Beppe's mother entered and asked, "Did you eat? Look at this skinny boy! Let me make some cappuccino." She swiftly sat me down in the dining room and filled a plate with fresh bread, ham, dry figs, wine, and homemade pastries baked earlier that morning.

After eating, I decided to rest for a couple hours, as my legs were cramped and tired from the ten-hour train ride. When I woke up, lunch was being prepared. It's difficult to estimate the number of people sitting at the table because there were second, third, and fourth cousins; and uncles, aunts, and neighbors. Maybe sixty? At the head of the table was the patriarch, Beppe's grandfather, the one who started it all. I sat right next to him. Everyone began talking to each other, but they were speaking the Barese dialect in such a way that I would've needed Google Translate to understand what they were saying.

Beppe's grandfather then said, "Let's speak some Italian; the poor guy doesn't understand a thing." They switched to formal Italian, and so I was able to be part of the conversation. Then the food came. There was seafood salad, eggplant and peppers, octopus, orecchiette with ragu, gnocchi with squid ink, and roast beef. I can't even remember all the dishes that were served. This was a unique experience that didn't even compare to the dinners at my own home. The bottles of wine were endless; and dried fruit, cakes, and limoncello gracefully ended the magnificent feast.

From the end of the table a man's voice came alive: "I am ready. Take me to bed." It was one of the grandfathers who had so much alcohol in his veins that he couldn't even get up from his chair. Some of the uncles picked him up and took him straight to bed, and as far as I know, he didn't move for two days.

My adventure in Bari was one of a kind. Food and love are two interchangeable concepts that you can always depend on in a family. Family is irreplaceable. I'm not usually someone who says *never*, but I can promise you: I will *never* eat at the Olive Garden. How could I?

Born as Soon as Possible

~⌒~

After nine months of being cramped in my mother's stomach, I was ready to shoot out like a Pop-Tart. I was excited. I needed to stretch and couldn't wait any longer. I had so many aspirations. I wanted to go to Disney World, sing my own version of "Stayin' Alive," and become a master of Michael Jackson's moonwalk.

It all began with my parents' vacation nine months before. I started out in my dad's pants, but it was my mom who brought me back home, as I had moved into the comfort of her egg. While my parents were resting after a long lovemaking session, I was part of an unforgettable race. There were millions of us squirming around. Exactly how many, I'm not sure, but it could have been as many as the population of Brazil. It was as if there were hordes of little beings coming from all over the country to Rio, to be part of the biggest celebration of the year—the Carnival that was going to happen inside this tiny little egg. Tickets weren't for sale, and to gain entrance to the exclusive party, we had to climb the fences. Only later would I know what that meant.

Before the race began, we were resting in the seminal vesicle, somewhere down in my dad's testicles. We were mostly identical, with a few exceptions—I think I saw a few with two heads and extra legs. But as we started running toward Rio, we showed our true colors, with some of us giving wrong directions or pushing without reason. It didn't take me too long to understand that this was no longer a friendly marathon among peers going to Rio, but a race to stay alive in the midst of such a hullabaloo. By the time I arrived in the uterus, I barely survived an ambush. Finally, I reached the fallopian freeway on my way to the Carnival. All I can say is that the egg must have liked me, as I gained entrance to my mother's exclusive villa, where I concluded my Armageddon.

During those nine long months, I was the main topic of conversation. My sister Gianna wanted to hear what I was up to and often placed her ear on our mother's stomach. For the first few months, I didn't have a clue what I looked like. But when I was three months along, I saw myself on television for the first time. I couldn't tell what channel I was on, but I could hear the doctor telling my parents that I was a boy, as my "thing" could be seen hanging in the water. Sorry! Next time I'll cover it up with my hands. It was then that my parents decided to call me Samuele. The doctor asked my parents if we were Jewish, because Samuele is an uncommon name for Italians. "No, we're not!" I shouted and kicked from inside. All I was concerned about was my little thing. "I'm Italian, and we don't do circumcisions in our country, thank you very much."

My mom did some clothes shopping, but not much. In fact, the bulk of my fancy pajamas came directly from the old wardrobe of my brothers: Filippo, who was ten years older; and Leonardo, who was six years older. They both had a passion for soccer. On Sundays I could hear them screaming when their favorite players were running on the soccer field. They would skip dinner if their team lost the match, as they were too upset to eat. But overall, their team, A.C. Milan, did well, better than the one I would later choose, A.C. Fiorentina. Growing up, my brothers would do all they could to convince me to change my soccer club, but I would always be a fan of Fiorentina.

When I was six months in the making, in the laboratory of my mother's body, my mom went back to the doctor, who again broadcast my picture on television. I was about two pounds at that point, and for the first time, I was able to see my toes and yes . . . my most precious hanging feature.

One day I felt myself falling. I was ready to be born! As Pinocchio would say, I was going to be a real boy and be part of this world. As the ninth month rolled in, I'd been cooked to perfection like a bean in pasta and fagioli. It was time to make it happen. I made a hole in the placenta. A few minutes later, I heard my mom yelling at my dad, "Giovanni, my water broke. Get me to the hospital now!" After nine months of a relatively calm environment, chaos began to set in. I wanted to be born as soon as possible. "Let's hurry. This baby is ready; he's pushing very hard," my mom added frantically.

My dad sped out of our driveway, and I felt that I might be born in the car. I could see the headlines now: "Baby Born at 90 Miles an Hour in a Brand-New Fiat." My mom made my dad push the gas pedal all the way down as they sped to the hospital, screaming, "This baby is in a rush; he's knocking me out. I'm going to deliver him right on this seat!" To which my dad responded, "Shove him back in. We're almost there. It's just a matter of passing a few more cars, including this BMW who's going to be surprised by my new Fiat Turbo Diesel." Luckily, there were no signs of the carabinieri, the highway patrol. It would have been cool if they'd shown up with sirens blazing, escorting us to the hospital like the Prime Minister of Italy.

We finally arrived at the hospital, where a group of nurses sat outside having their smoke break. They dropped their cigarettes and helped roll my mom onto a bed as fast as a tire change in Formula 1, and they pushed all the way to the 100-meter finish line in the delivery room. The doctor was steadily poised, ready to catch me, much like a goalie during a penalty. Was he really the doctor, or was he Dino Zoff, who helped the Italian team win the World Cup in 1982?

I was born on the evening of July 5, 1971. I screamed, "I'm here! I made it!" One of the nurses declared that I'd been the fastest delivery in my hometown, even breaking some Olympic record. But my looks were rather unexpected. And suddenly the room was quiet. My dad came closer to look at me and asked, "Are we sure this is my son? His hair reminds me of a punk! And what's that? Is it a nose? He looks like an abstract painting Picasso might have drawn after taking some suspicious pills in Ibiza." My poor dad! Fathers are so worried, and they don't realize that the delivery is quite an effort for the mother as well as the baby, who must get through that little hole into the light of this world. It's like pushing an elephant through the door of a living room, thousands of people pushing his bottom, and then by some miracle, landing on top of the sofa without breaking the walls or scaring the cat.

For mothers it's a different story. In Italian, we say: "A little one is never ugly to their mom"—even if the baby looks like a *scarrafone*, or a cockroach, which may sound a bit harsh in English. Mothers have no doubt that their babies will be chosen for a Gerber commercial, be a top model for Valentino or Prada, or become the most accomplished player for Real Madrid or FC Barcelona.

My aunt Beatrice said, "Ugly in birth, beautiful in the plaza," which is an Italian way of offering some relief to the rest of the family, who are worried about the baby's looks. According to this saying, if the baby is indeed ugly at birth, his beauty will blossom with time, and he'll walk through the plaza with everyone turning around to admire him. The comments about newborns are endless. Some will see beauty in the chin that resembles the grandmother, or the eyes just like Great-Aunt Pina. Or how a spacious forehead, like the pampas in Argentina, is a clear sign that the baby will be a nuclear engineer or a brilliant physician.

While people were talking around me and making remarks about my cheeks, eyebrows, and nose, I was sucking my mom's milk, which tasted amazing and was coming from the best-shaped container. It felt good to hold it in my little hands. My father came to give me a second look. "On second thought, he is very cute. Look at how he likes to suck on that breast. He likes the good stuff, and I can tell he's going to be smart. One day he'll be someone important and make me a proud father. He is my Samuelino, little Samuele. I will call him Lele." However, my dad had to change his mind about my being a "little" Samuele when he changed my first diaper. I'm sure it wasn't a pretty scene, and he was probably wondering how I could have created so much pollution in my diaper. He must have asked himself, "What is this? Nuclear waste? What does he eat to make his waste so green? Is it pepperoni or asparagus or algae from the sea?"

This is how I came into the world. I wanted to be born right away, and I almost did in my dad's brand-new Turbo Diesel Fiat. Now that I'm older, I laugh with my mom and dad, remembering that day—the day I came into the world pushing and screaming . . . in a hurry to be born as soon as possible.

Catechism

The First Communion is a traditional Catholic ceremony in which a person receives his or her first Eucharist, or the Body of Christ. This is an important rite of passage because the Eucharist occupies a central role in Catholic theology and practice. It occurs only after receiving the blessing of baptism, and when the person has reached an age of reason—in my case, once I turned eight. When the priest told me that I'd reached the age of reason, I thought I was so cool. I bragged about it for weeks. But the priest made it clear that I was no exception, as the other kids had also reached that milestone.

I wanted to tell him, "Thanks for letting me know—now that I've made a complete egotistical fool of myself."

I don't know how the Catholic Church determines that eight is the moment when unreasonable people become reasonable. Sometimes I feel unreasonable even now that I've passed the venerable age of forty. I've read countless articles and studies that conclude that the age of eight is when most reason is lost to parental and social influences. But maybe the Church meant something else when it talked about reason. Since First Confession (the first sacrament of penance) must precede the First Communion, reaching the age of reason could mean recognizing one's own sins, and the need to ask for forgiveness. It's the basis of Church Fundamentals 101:

you recognize yourself as a sinner, pay the annual dues, and become an all-inclusive member of the club.

Before I received my First Communion, I had to attend three months of Saturday-afternoon classes at my parish to learn every concept of the Christian doctrine in great depth. The class was run by a priest, who with great patience tried to explain their newly acquired reason to us children and how to make sense of Jesus's teachings. The class would start with a prayer followed by the signing of the cross: "In the name of the Father, the Son, and the Holy Spirit." From the very beginning, I was quite inquisitive. For example, I felt that the Holy Spirit was a sort of intruder. What was he doing there with the Father and the Son, and why did he take it upon himself to break the family apart? What happened to the Mother? Why couldn't the Mother be a part of the family? She was the one who'd delivered Baby Jesus and cared for him since Christmas day. I didn't remember the Holy Spirit in the nativity replica at my parents' house. Why did *he* suddenly get to have the spotlight?

I had another problem with the Holy Spirit. After dinner, my grandma would often disappear into the living room without explanation. One day I asked her, "Grandma, where are you going?"

She replied, "Stay there, I'll be right back. I'm going to get some Spirit." So, the next day when the priest asked the class if we knew what the Holy Spirit was, I raised my hand.

The priest said, "Go ahead, Samuele. Please tell the class what you know about the Holy Spirit."

I replied, "I've never *seen* the Holy Spirit, but I know that my grandma sees it every night after dinner."

"Samuele, please don't lie to the class about your grandma Bruna. How can she see the Holy Spirit every night after dinner? The Holy Spirit is invisible."

"But my grandma told me so. And when she comes back from the living room, she's very happy. She also told me that the Holy Spirit is good for the digestion."

"What else did she tell you?" the priest asked.

"That if you give the Holy Spirit to some people, they'll tell you their secrets. On one occasion, I heard my dad asking, 'Who finished the bottle of spirit?' Turns out, it was my grandma."

Eventually, I learned that the spirit my grandma spoke of was very different from that which my priest was referring to. However, in my opinion, they do have a few similarities. They both make people act strange, make them speak different languages, and say truths that they otherwise would never admit. The Holy Spirit is also called "the Spirit of Truth," which correlates to the Latin phrase *in vino veritas*, meaning, "When you drink wine, you speak the truth." Spirit was also helpful in making people sing and rejoice. The only major difference was that one was sitting in the alcohol cupboard of my living room, and the other was part of the Holy Trinity alongside the Father and the Son—but not the Mother. According to the Gospels of Matthew and Luke, Jesus was conceived by the Holy Spirit and born of the Virgin Mary. Therefore, he was legitimately part of the family. But I still wished they would have shoved the Mother into the equation. After all, she's the one who had to give birth.

In the next class, the priest taught us about the book of Genesis, which explains how the world came about. "In the beginning, God created the heavens and the earth." As an eight-year-old, I found the beginning of the Bible rather monotonous. Personally, I would have started the story very differently. Obviously, I was only a child, so what could I know about complex matters such as religion and doctrine? There had to be a good reason why the first chapter of the Bible began that way. Despite the lousy beginning, the Bible was a bestseller, a good sign that people liked it the way it was written. I, on the other hand, liked to read science-fiction books and watch *Star Trek*. My favorite cartoon was *The Jetsons*, the space equivalent to *The Flintstones*. In my imaginative mind, I envisioned the Genesis starting in a more exciting way. . . .

Adam and Eve were traveling through the Milky Way with their aero car, a flying saucer with a transparent bubble top. They'd departed from their planet, Orbit City, the same one inhabited by the Jetsons. It was a few days after their wedding on Orbit City, and they were on their honeymoon.

"Adam, we're lost in space. Where are we?"

"Eve, I though you downloaded the directions. The power-generator signal is flashing. We're losing plutonic energy . . ."

"Did you get the Apple?"

"You mean the iPhone?"

"Yeah, the iPhone."

"The intergalactic line isn't working. I may have forgotten to pay the bill on time."

"We're going down. Get the parachutes. We're headed directly toward that blue planet."

Years later, Adam and Eve created a home for themselves on the foreign planet, using the trees and stones around them. They were never able to contact Orbit City, thus leaving them no other option but to start a new life on what they called "Earth." They had two children, Cain and Abel. The brothers were complete opposites. Cain was nervous and irritable; and Abel was happy, enthusiastic, and a child of the flowers. Cain often went hunting with his father, while Abel preferred staying home with his mother to garden and take care of the sheep. As a teenager, Cain began acting irrationally and was always frustrated. One night he shaved, combed his hair, sprayed himself with some Aqua di Gió; then he covered himself with a nice, decorated new leaf.

"Mother, I'm going out tonight."

"Cain, it'll be dark soon. Come back before dawn or you'll get lost in Eden."

"Mom, stop worrying. I must find what I need most. If I find myself in the right situation . . . I won't be back tonight."

Eve knew that Cain was growing and that his testosterone was kicking in. She was sympathetic to her son's frustrations, but there was nothing she could do about it. She'd told him about the disastrous crash of the aero car and that they didn't have a way to get back home. In Orbit City, Cain could have had a normal life and even a girlfriend by now. Here on Earth, however, there were no signs of other humans. Cain explored every square inch of the Garden of Eden, but to no avail. One day he saw a black smog strip in the sky. He ran to see what it was. At the base of a tree were the smoking remains of a spaceship, with no other sign of life.

"Anybody there? Hello?" Cain kept calling. "It's safe. Please come out, whoever you are. I'm here to help you." Suddenly, from a nearby bush, four people appeared: a man, a woman and . . . two girls. And, thank you, Lord, to Cain's delight, the two girls were not lesbians.

And that is how humankind came to be.

My story may not have been as dramatic as the one the priest taught us, but I preferred it. God didn't get upset about Eve's betrayal with the forbidden fruit, Abel didn't die, and

Cain became a good husband and father for humankind. I'm not sure about Abel. He may not have had the same ambitions as Cain, but I'm certain the other girl was able to convince him or clear his mind of any doubts.

We kept reading the Bible and reached the story of Noah.

Scientists have estimated that 90 percent of the world's species have become extinct. I can't imagine how hard life must have been for people at the beginning. Adam and Eve probably had to make a big adjustment from the comfort of Orbit City to the wilderness of Earth at the dawn of civilization. They must have fought every day with millions of insects and animals. Their mornings likely began very early, with thousands of roosters waking everyone at 3 a.m. One would have to fight piranhas and unfriendly fish jumping from the water as they tried to bathe. A daily walk in the wilderness would cause constant stress, given the presence of many ferocious animals and the unexpected bowel movements of the birds in the trees.

Gathering fruits and vegetables wasn't easy, as many were infested with worms. As soon as people put down their leaf covers to relieve themselves, their butts would be targets for flies and mosquitoes. It was impossible to sleep because of the strong light from the fireflies, like the displays in Times Square. By the time someone fell asleep, the roosters would start up again with their cock-a-doodle-doos and so on and so forth. It's no wonder that humans saw insects and most animals as annoyances. They were stressed by the animals, which inspired their negative behaviors with each other, causing many pointless fights and deaths. To give the world a clean slate, God caused a universal flood. Why? It wasn't humans' fault that the situation had degenerated. It was the animals' fault. And what did God decide to do? He saved the animals, killed all the men and women, and started humanity from scratch with the help of Noah.

To say that Noah was a man of patience would be an understatement. He had to build an ark and then make sure each species had a male and female representative on board. If Noah had known what this job entailed beforehand, I'm sure he would have thought twice about submitting his résumé. One might ask, how did he distinguish between a male and a female ant? Is the little thing big enough to be seen with naked eyes? He also had to make sure that the anteater cell was on the opposite side of the ark. And the termites . . . let's not forget the termites. They had to be placed in a special container due to their affinity for the wood of the ark. Finally, everybody was enlisted and ready to board with the proper paperwork, except for a few dozen sly foxes that had managed to make some fake passports and sneak in illegally. The ark was in motion, while rain poured nonstop.

It could have been the rain, the cold, or the fact that all the animals were together in one boat, but they all began to copulate with each other, running back and forth on the ark, some to escape from animals that preferred to swing with different partners. What can you say about the poor ostrich that would often put his head down and leave his back unprotected, leaving himself open to the unrestrained hormones of the orangutan? The zebra was running away from the horse, the female horse from the donkey, and the llama from the chimpanzee. The praying mantis had to refrain from her instinctive inclination to kill her husband after having sex, and the snail was undecided on which of her male and female reproductive organs to use. Meanwhile, Noah had to stay in his cabin, as he was annoyed by the feigning innocence of the bleating sheep that would swing by every time the ram was asleep. When the rain stopped, Noah even considered killing off the mosquito species because of the various unwelcome bites he received. But he couldn't let them go extinct!

For an eight-year-old, and a "man of reason," I thought that God had overreacted to the misbehavior of human beings. I couldn't understand why He would create so much stress for poor Noah, the animal kingdom, and the entire human race, who probably would have repented with a Father-son talk face-to-face. I had a better solution to this mess and would have volunteered to do my part. This was my plan:

> The universal punishment would start at my home, in the kitchen. I'd put a pot of water on the stove to boil. I'd throw the pasta in the pot and sauté it with some carbonara sauce. But the pasta would begin growing and growing without stopping. I had begun the Universal Flood of Pasta. God would then yell from his megaphone:

> "Men and woman of Earth, you have given me much pain by refusing to take care of each other and the animals. But I am a forgiving Father and ready to give you another chance before I send you my son—I know he will have to come sooner or later. You must eat all the pasta, until the last string, and I don't want excuses. Be quiet and eat. This is your fate!"

> Humankind began the enormous task of eating the pasta. In the beginning, the pasta carbonara tasted good, but day after day, the men and women felt heavy and blown up. They had severe stomach pains, nausea, and diarrhea. It took humankind a long time to clear the planet from the pasta, but they finally did, and exhaustedly went to God.

> "We don't want to eat or see pasta for thousands of years."

> "That's fine," replied God. "I hope you have all learned a lesson, and support and respect each other. I love you, and I hope you know that I did this for your own good."

> "Sure, God, but please hide the pasta."

"Okay. I will hide it in China."

So, God taught a lesson to all humankind, avoided a flooding mess, and everybody was happy and in peace with each other and the animals. Humans didn't eat pasta for thousands of years, until it was rediscovered in China and imported to Italy.

Obviously, I didn't tell my story to the priest. But how cool it would have been if the Bible had offered that alternative. . . .

What Happened to Bernabo?

When I think about my grandmother, I always get a smile on my face. She was born on May 6, 1898, in Vaiano, a small village in Tuscany. She was one of eleven children. I remember one day, on her birthday, my family took a picture of her, her older sister, and her brother. We added up the ages of the three together and almost got a combined three hundred years. My grandmother died at the age of ninety-three. She went to the hospital very few times in her life, but then, at the beginning of 1991, she started having issues with her stomach; and in May, she was hospitalized with a tumor diagnosis. She could have had an operation, but I think the doctor just let her go. It was very quick. In a matter of three weeks, she got very sick and then died.

During her funeral service, the casket was left open. There were hundreds of people at the ceremony, and one by one, each of them got the opportunity to bid her goodbye for the last time before she was buried at the cemetery. But I didn't. I was too sad to see her go. I didn't want my last memory of her to be in a casket with her eyes closed. Her spirit remained with me, as well as her smile. She had such an enthusiasm for people and life, a love for me and her other grandchildren.

I was the fourth in my family. I slept in my parents' room until I was three. When my little sister was born, my parents had to find space for the crib in their room. There was a lack of vacant rooms with such a big family. Therefore, I ended up sharing a room with my grandmother, who also lived with us. My grandmother and I were roommates until I was eleven years old, and we had a very special bond. At night, before going to sleep, we would say a prayer together. Other times, she would tell me stories about her childhood, and how she grew up on a farm with her brothers and sisters. She taught me the many customs and history of Tuscany. I can't remember every story, but one that always remains with me is that of Jesus and Peter traveling around the world. It was a folktale that was funny, surreal, and moralistic. The story begins with a question: *Where are Jesus and Peter traveling today?* Tuscany is not such a bad place to hang out. It has delicious food, good wine, and beautiful scenery. And here they are, Jesus and Peter, wandering around in my beloved Tuscany.

> So, one day, Jesus and Peter were walking on the Via Francigena toward San Gimignano. They had walked for a long time and decided to take a little rest on a field. It was almost time for lunch, and they were hungry. They hadn't found anybody along the road to offer them a meal or a place to rest. While walking, Jesus was quiet, but Peter kept mumbling. Next to the field, Peter saw a group of big trees and asked, "Jesus, what are those trees?"

> "Those are walnut trees, Peter," said Jesus.

> "Are they good to eat?" asked Peter.

> "Yes, they are," responded Jesus.

Peter harvested some of the walnuts and cracked them open. He ate thirty of them and then rested in the grass.

Peter asked, "My Lord, did you invent walnuts?"

"Of course, Peter, I invented everything. Why?"

"I was just thinking. Sometimes I don't understand you. You always seem to want to do things your way."

"What do you mean, Peter?"

"I am talking about the walnuts."

"Don't you like them?"

"Yes, Jesus. I thought they were very good."

"Then what is the problem?"

"What I don't understand is why you made the walnuts so small. You see, I had to crack thirty of them to feel satisfied, and it was a lot of unnecessary work. Think about the poor farmers who come home, tired after a long day's work in the field. Do you think they have the energy to open thirty walnuts? Couldn't you have made the walnuts bigger? That way it would take less time for them to become satiated."

Jesus didn't respond to Peter. He knew Peter too well to give him a response, but Jesus still liked him, despite all his flaws. After taking a little afternoon nap under the trees, the two men continued their journey. Then, suddenly, the wind started blowing hard, and the tree branches started swaying. A walnut fell on Peter's head.

"Damn, that had to fall right on my head? It really hurts."

Jesus told him, "Think how painful it would have been if the walnut was as big as you suggested."

Now, Peter understood that Jesus had a point in having made things the way they are.

Jesus and Peter continued to walk to Volterra, another beautiful town in Tuscany, the cradle of the Etruscan civilization. As they walked, they met many farmers who expressed their unhappiness with the weather. Some were wishing for more sunshine, others complained about the wind, and some weren't satisfied with the precipitation during winter. Peter was very upset that the farmers were unhappy, but Jesus wasn't responding to them. Peter thought that Jesus was being unfair.

"Jesus, I cannot believe that you are ignoring these farmers. If I were you, I would be a little more understanding and give them sun, rain, and wind when they ask for it. I would try to accommodate their needs to the best of my ability."

"Peter, maybe you should take charge of the weather responsibilities. Go ahead. From now on, *you* make the decisions," Jesus said.

Peter went to the farmers and asked them what type of weather they preferred. First, they asked for rain. The next day they asked for sun. Peter was happy to please the farmers. Then it came time for the harvest. The farmers weren't happy with their crops. The seeds of the grain were empty, and the fruit of the trees was not as juicy as the year before. It had rained when there was no need for rain. There was sun when there was no need for sun. And nobody had asked for wind, which was necessary for the growth of the crops. The farmers suffered a very scarce harvest for the entire year. Now, Peter understood that Jesus had a point in limiting the farmers' desires, because they didn't know what weather was needed for the prosperity of their lands. Jesus took back the responsibility, and the next harvest was plentiful.

As they continued their journey, Peter and Jesus arrived at a beautiful church and stopped to attend the Mass. Once inside, they couldn't find a place to sit because the church was full of people listening to the preacher's sermon, which went on for quite a while. Everyone in the room was mesmerized by his words of wisdom. At the end of the service, Jesus approached the preacher to thank him for such a wonderful sermon, which encouraged people to endure every obstacle in good spirits. Peter, however, was not of the same opinion.

"Jesus, if you only knew who that preacher was, you wouldn't be praising him. He's a great sinner, and he does the opposite of what he preaches. You wouldn't want to have anything to do with him. I cannot believe that you like a person who is so hypocritical. I would never want to be in his company."

Jesus didn't respond and continued walking. After some time, Peter became thirsty but couldn't find a source of water. He started complaining incessantly.

"I'm so thirsty. I don't know what I would do for a pint of water. But there's no water here. It's so hot and sticky."

"Peter, there's plenty of water here," replied Jesus.

"Jesus, I don't know where you see water."

"Peter, just go down that path behind the hill and you'll find a little creek."

Peter followed Jesus's directions and came back satisfied, with his face refreshed.

"Thank you, Jesus, you were right. There *was* water. I've never had water that good in my life. It was so satisfyingly light."

"I'm glad to hear that. But Peter, did you see where the water was coming from? Go back and walk to the top of the creek."

Peter went back and saw that the water was coming out of the body of a dead animal. He returned to Jesus, completely disgusted.

"Jesus, I cannot believe what I saw. The water was coming out of a dead body."

"I know, Peter. But didn't you like the water? I made sure that the water was safe, even if it was from a bad source. The same can be said for that preacher. He may be a sinner, and he may be hypocritical, but his words were inspiring, and many good deeds can result from people who listen to his message. Let us not judge him. Let us take the positive from any experience and leave the rest to God."

> Peter understood this lesson and continued his
> journey through Tuscany with Jesus.

My grandmother was very religious. She went to church every Sunday and holiday, but she never imposed her opinions on others, and never took the words of the Bible literally. She also liked to have a glass of wine with every meal. Indeed, my father always discovered that his favorite bottle of liquor was empty. She would drink a small glass every night after dinner to aid her digestion. She always encouraged trying everything in moderation. For Lent, she would abstain from alcohol out of respect. Regarding sacrifice, my grandmother would always tell me the story of Bernabo.

> Bernabo was a young man who lived with his parents in the countryside in the region of Chianti. He was a talented violinist. My grandma told me that his fame had reached her town when she was a little girl. Sometimes he would accompany a group of traveling dancers who performed at the annual Carnival, the period of festivities that lead to Lent. It was rather scandalous to organize a dancing gig during this religious holiday because it was considered a time for repentance and prayer.
>
> The night of Ash Wednesday, the first day of Lent, Bernabo had just finished dinner with his parents. He grabbed his violin and proceeded to walk out the door. Before leaving, his father reminded him that nobody should be hanging out in public that night. Instead, people were going to spend time with their families. Bernabo, however, refuted the customs of Lent and said rather defiantly, "I want to play my violin, and Lent or no Lent, I'm going to find someone to dance with me tonight. Even if it means that

I'll be dancing with the devil." As he turned to leave, Bernabo's parents sighed heavily and made the sign of the cross.

Bernabo went from village to village to find people willing to dance to his music, but every house was closed, and the streets were empty out of respect for Lent. He finally found a man along a crossroad.

"Hello, sir, my name is Bernabo. I'm looking for a place where I can play my violin."

"You can come to my house. I'm having a big party tonight," the man said.

Suddenly, a strong gust of wind raised the surrounding leaves on the floor in a tornado-like whirl, and Bernabo found himself in a dance saloon, in the middle of a crowd. There was excessive drinking, dancing, and music. Bernabo began to play his violin, and everyone crowded around him to dance. Meanwhile, the air inside the saloon was getting heavy and unbreathable. Bernabo realized that the place didn't have windows, except for a small opening at the back of the room. He looked through the opening and saw his uncle, who had died sometime before.

His uncle looked up and asked, "What are you doing here?"

"Hello, Uncle, I'm here to play some music and entertain."

"Bernabo, you're a fool. You're in hell, and the man who invited you to come is the devil. You need to run away from here as soon as you can."

"But how can I? I don't see any way out of here."

"You need to pray to the crucifix of the Holy Face and repent for what you did."

Bernabo was scared, but he listened to his uncle. Then, another whirl of wind brought him back to the crossroad where he'd met the man. Fearful and cold, he ran home and told his parents what had happened. He vowed never again to play the violin during Lent.

My grandma added at the end of the story, "All is good, all is holy. There is a time for everything, especially when thanking God, for keeping you healthy and happy."

I am so thankful to God for giving me my grandmother, for whom I have the fondest memories. Every time I think of her, I feel the warmth of her smiling face.

Politics and Religion?
No, Thanks!

ॐ

*W*hen I moved to the United States, I was told to follow one simple rule: avoid talking about politics or religion. I found this rule interesting because in Italy it's *all* we talk about, aside from food and women. So why do Americans avoid it? It seems that their motivation is to prevent annoying and litigious arguments that, from the perspective of a typical Italian, are the key reasons for a conversation: make arguments and possibly argue until one is exhausted from doing so.

When I lived in Rignano sull'Arno, a small village in Italy, I would walk to the local café after dinner to get a digestive liqueur and converse with the people in the square. During election time—which is almost year-round, considering that Italy has had more than sixty governments since 1948—the people at the café would be having heated conversations about the new candidates or parties on the ballot. In fact, every election would bring forth a new group claiming that *they* were the ones who were going to perform a permanent face-lift on the old political "fresco." Their promise was to bring sanity and a new era of change to the nation.

From one section of the café to the other, comments and counterarguments were shouted out: "Down with the chauvinists!" "When Mussolini was alive, the trains were on time!" "I'm voting for Cicciolina!" and more and more, because politics is the cause of endless discussion that, in Italy, becomes just folkloristic debate. There is an endless ocean between the saying and the doing. At the end of the night, no matter what argument was undertaken by two opposite sides, everyone would hug each other, and all was forgotten; and even what wasn't forgotten was considered an opinion to be respected. Arguments and opinions could never break the friendships and solidarity among people of the same village. Brotherhood came before everything else.

A glimpse of the reality of Italian politics was depicted in a series of books and movies from the 1950s with an imaginary character, Don Camillo. He was the idealistic parish priest of a small village in the north of Italy, postwar. Don Camillo wasn't a mild-mannered priest just out of the seminary, but rather a corpulent man who often resorted to feats of physical strength to solve issues that at first seemed impossible to untangle. Don Camillo also spoke directly with the Christ depicted in the crucifix at the altar, who advised him on which courses of action to take. (Even God was involved in the politics of Italy.) In fact, Don Camillo was a politicized priest committed to the Christian Democratic Party and who disapproved of communist ideology. Another character, Mayor Peppone, was head of the local section of the Communist Party. Divided by opposing ideologies, the two protagonists had to put aside their differences and work side by side when the safety of the village was in danger.

During the '80s and '90s, Italy had seen the creation of some of the most unprofessional political parties with imaginative names and seemingly impossible goals. The époque of this "Everybody gets their own party" movement has now ended. The current political scene is dominated by a few gregarious Left and Right coalitions. The party of "Hunting and Fishing," "The Rainbow," "Housewives," and the "Love Party" are significant contributors to Italian political history. If people feel like talking about politics in Italy, they can join the club, have some laughs. If the laugh becomes an argument, there's no need to worry: it's all good, because in Italy, there aren't any rules when it comes to politics and politicians. Very little seems to have changed from the time of the Romans in that sense. Of course, we no longer have Nero and Caligula, but as far as funny business goes, there's still plenty on the political scene.

On the other end, when it comes to religion, one cannot say the topic is completely open to argument if it's contrary to Christian beliefs. Rome has been the center of Christianity for two thousand years, as well as home to the Pope, Jesus's Viceroy on Earth, since the Apostle Peter funded the Catholic Church. However, as the Catholic Church has continued to be the most dominant presence, other religions have taken root in the Pope's country. Not too long ago, the Inquisition run by the Jesuits would have condemned any deviation from the norm. But today, even Scientology has a branch office next to Saint Peter's Cathedral. Buddha, Krishna, Vishnu, and Zoroaster are no longer mysterious entities to be feared as the concoction of witches.

Today, Florence is home to one of the largest communities of Jehovah's Witnesses, although I never had the pleasure of meeting any of them when I lived in Italy. When they would knock on the door of our house, my annoyed mom would open the door and tell them to leave. I couldn't believe how rude she was to them; this didn't reflect the spirit of my family, who were always so welcoming to anybody who came to our home. No sign of affection or even minimal understanding was ever given to the members of this mysterious religion. They were talking about Jesus, so why was my mother so upset with them? She could have at least let them come in for a cup of coffee and a piece of her apple cake.

When I was older, I decided to ask her about it. I said, "Mom, why were you so unwelcoming to the Jehovah's Witnesses?"

My mom promptly responded, "Because they don't let their people have blood transfusions, even if they are suffering and dying."

"Transfusions?" I asked. "Mom, the French eat frogs and snails, but we still talk to *them*. It's their choice. Could we at least offer them a glass of wine? Wine is good for blood circulation."

But my mom wasn't convinced, "No, you don't understand. They would rather harm their children in order to adhere to their beliefs. And where did they get this rule? Certainly not in the Bible. They're not coming in my house. I would rather cook snails and frogs for the French Foreign Legion."

My mom had a point. Why were the Jehovah's Witnesses against modern medicine? God believed in medicine. When Moses went to Mount Sinai to get the Ten Commandments, God saw poor, feverish Moses and told him, "Take these two tablets. Don't forget to swallow them with some water."

It wasn't until I came to San Diego that I could finally open my home to the Jehovah's Witnesses and get a sense of what they were all about. The first couple that came to my house didn't have much to say, but I let them in and offered them some coffee, to their surprise. They confessed that they had never gone so far, meaning they'd never crossed the entrance of someone's home. The most they'd been able to accomplish until that point was to stand in front of the door and distribute their pamphlets. But no, I'd actually let them in. We all sat down in the living room, drinking coffee. They weren't trained on what to do in this type of situation. But they must have taken it seriously, because they sent two new faces a few weeks later.

"Good morning," I said to the two men standing in front of me. One was tall and the other chunky, but both were dressed in jackets and ties.

"Buongiorno," they responded, with a slight Italian accent.

"You speak Italian?"

"Yes, we do. We are Jehovah's Witnesses. I think you met two of our members a few weeks ago."

"Yes, I remember."

"Well, we belong to the same congregation. In fact, we have several Italians in our church, and my niece is married to one of them."

"Well, I'm sorry for your niece. I hope she's doing okay. Please come in. Welcome to my home."

It was Saturday morning, and I had some time on my hands. I was curious to find out more about their religion. Besides the fact that they seemed more prepared than the previous individuals who'd come to my door, they also spoke Italian. This was going to be quite interesting. I prepared coffee, and one of them even suggested some tips on how to make it creamier. Amazing! Did they get this information from their Bible? Then we discussed the meaning of life and the Armageddon coming upon us. I had to tell them that it had already happened many times, at least every time we had political elections in Italy. They were a little pessimistic about the world, but I really enjoyed the conversation. But they kept coming back over the following months, and they would take out the Bible immediately. They would try to teach me about things that I'd heard many times growing up in my church, but they claimed that *their* Bible translation was the most accurate.

Eventually, the lessons started to get a bit annoying, and I missed that reciprocal aspect of having a different opinion. I had the feeling that after the introduction, they were moving into a new phase: recruitment and the offering of salvation. It was then that I had to use a special trick to make them disappear. The following weekend, just before they took out their Bible, I told them to wait while I went to get something. When I returned, I slammed a book on the table and yelled: "Voilà!" It was a gastronomic cookbook, with seventeen hundred recipes from all over the world. I told them that the book summarized the essence of living.

"Gentlemen, this is *my* Bible," I told them as I opened the cookbook to show them the pictures of traditional peasant recipes including octopus, chickpeas, asparagus, and boiled beets.

"What is it?"

"It's a cookbook."

"How can a collection of recipes for brussel sprouts be a Holy Book?"

"This book speaks about the wedding of Florence, where Jesus transformed house wine into Brunello of Montalcino and the multiplication of pizzas in Naples. The message of Jesus in this cookbook is the same as the Bible."

"I would have to disagree," said the tall guy, the most adamant one.

I said, "*Everything* is sacred. What's the difference between the smallest particle of your body and the one of a star?"

"If you don't repent and follow Jehovah, you cannot reach that star and go to heaven."

"Let me think about it. But how about next time you invite me to *your* house for a coffee?"

"We cannot invite nonmembers to our homes," he replied.

"You see, that is not the spirit of *my* cookbook."

"What do you mean?" he asked.

I told him, "My religion states that after eating and drinking, we all have to go to the bathroom and sit on the toilet. From the greatest statesmen to the Pope, from Bombay to Costa Rica, we are all brothers and sisters in the name of the bathroom."

"That's not what we believe in."

"I can see that you don't believe in that. Well, that's all the time I can give you today. I have some cooking to do. Thanks for coming. See you at your house, upon your invitation. By the way, it doesn't seem like you needed an invitation from *me* to come to *my* house."

They've never called me back or invited me over. I guess my crap wasn't holy enough for their toilets.

Arguing is the lifeblood of the Italian people, who can admit that there are things beyond the Bible, such as blood transfusions. But after my experience with the Jehovah's Witnesses, I learned again that there's a time to be open to any type of conversation and a time to cut it short when it's no longer based on reciprocal respect. In any family, there should be room for agreement and disagreement. If one cannot agree on this simple rule, then others are free to disagree, but they're also welcome to leave me alone, thank you very much.

As far as I was concerned, I was done with the Jehovah's Witnesses. I couldn't accept the fact that there was no salvation for my soul, especially considering their narrow terms. In fact, if I *had* joined their group, I would have still needed to get in line right behind the last one to join the club before me and hope to win the lottery to heaven. According to their Bible, there's a select number of spots in heaven, about 140,000. How could I have beaten the millions in front of me? I had better odds of standing in the airport in Dubai with seventy-two virgins waiting to be delivered to Allah. Good luck to the last guy joining right before the Armageddon! Becoming a Jehovah's Witness defeated even the mathematical equation of Blaise Pascal, who said that it's better to believe than not to believe: one has a fifty-fifty chance to be right about what happens after death and go straight to heaven. Apparently, he didn't know that some religions have a VIP list!

Lost at Sea

When I was little, my father rented a house for our family so we could spend the summer at the beach. Our vacation home was about an hour away from Florence, not too far for my father to join the family during the weekends, as he couldn't take the entire summer off from work. He had his own business, a textile company, and he had to keep the machines running. On the other hand, my mom, my siblings, and my grandmother had the chance to spend time away from home, where it was often too hot and humid during the summer. We rented the same house several times during my childhood. The village we stayed in was called Forte dei Marmi. My older sister, Gianna, and my two brothers, Filippo and Leonardo, had made some friends during these many summers. My sister Sara was three years younger than I was, and she stayed with my mother at the beach house, as she was too small to venture out on her own.

During most weekends, we had visitors. My great-aunt Bice and great-uncle Giulio would spend a few weeks with us each summer. The house had many rooms, so there was always a place for our guests to stay overnight. Almost every morning, my mom went to the bakery and brought home fresh schiacchiata, a flat, salted bread, as well as Tuscan bread. We would all gather in the kitchen for breakfast and have warm milk and coffee. Then we got ready to go down to the sea, where we'd rented a few umbrellas and beach chairs for the family. Fortunately, the beach was only a few blocks away from our home. My mom joined us in the afternoon, because she first had to tend to the laundry and clean the house, because of all the sand that we dragged inside from our feet and clothes the day before.

My older sister and brother rarely stayed with us because they had their own plans with their friends. So, most of the time I played with my other brother, Leonardo, making sandcastles or flicking plastic balls in the sand. Every morning, before taking a swim in the sea, we had specific instructions to wait until two hours after breakfast to digest our food. So for two hours my brother and I would sit on the sand playing, and every ten minutes we asked, "Is it time yet? Can we go in the sea?" Finally, the tedious hours passed, and we would run to the beach and splash in the water.

One day my great-aunt Bice, my brother Leonardo, and I walked to the Bagno Santa Maria, a sort of beach club, where we had our umbrella. As usual, my great-aunt sat reading and tanning, while my brother and I played together. After some time, my great-aunt asked my brother where I was, because I'd disappeared.

Indeed, I *had* disappeared, and my brother didn't know where. Where could I have possibly gone? I might have walked home to get something, but that would have been quite unusual, as I was only four years old. Then, my great-aunt told my brother to check the house, but she reminded him not to tell our mother that I was missing. If my mother knew what was going on, she would surely begin panicking. My brother was instructed to look around and come back to the umbrella if he couldn't find me. My brother went home to look for me in the yard, in my room, as well as the rooms upstairs. Eventually my mom saw him and asked him why he'd come home, and more important, why he wasn't with me. Mothers have a unique sixth sense where they can feel that something is wrong. She asked him, "Did something happen?" And then my brother felt the pressure to spill the beans, replying, "We lost Samuele!"

My mother isn't known to be a very athletic person, but when she heard the news, she ran so fast that I'm sure she broke a couple of records. She was at the beach within minutes, and twenty people were trying to calm her down. They promised to help find me. It was a matter of sending a dispatch to all the other establishments on the coast, giving them a description of me, and the bystanders assured my mother that everything was going to be okay. It took some time, but finally my mom calmed down a bit. However, she insisted on the involvement of the police, the carabinieri, the Red Cross, firefighters, and the civil protection agency. She also threatened to call the president of Italy. Eventually, after an hour, they found me three kilometers north of Bagno Santa Maria. I was walking on the beach, following, at a short distance, a man. This man was no ordinary man, though, but somebody rather special, at least for me.

On the beach in Italy, there are many vendors. Some sell food; others sell clothes or handmade garments. The man I was following had his face painted like a clown, and he was selling balloons. He had a hundred colorful, inflated balloons, just like you'd see at the entrance of a carnival or a circus. I was probably wondering how he could walk instead of floating away with all those balloons. As I followed him, I never took my eyes off those balloons. I still have many memories from that day. I was completely unaware that I'd caused so much commotion in my family. Indeed, I was quite surprised that I'd just walked through the wet sand of Forte dei Marmi, following the footsteps of a face-painted man with colorful balloons.

Perhaps it was this experience that set in motion my curiosity, affirming my interest in exploring and traveling the world. Maybe the vision of happiness and joy that this man brought to the kids he encountered caused me to follow him for three kilometers. It took so little, just a few balloons, to

45

make people happy and smile. Whatever it was, that moment of my childhood still lives in my mind and gives me comfort and the willingness to never stop enjoying the journey of life — just like that day at the sea, under the sun, with the curiosity of my four-year-old self.

Crosswords, Anagrams, and Frats

*n every town in Italy, there's a kiosk that sells newspapers and magazines. People can also subscribe to their favorite periodicals and receive them in the mail. My father, however, preferred to do things the old-fashioned way. He enjoyed a nice walk through the neighborhood and conversed with the locals. This was also a way for him and my mom to get a little break from each other. For many years, he would buy a crossword-puzzle magazine to keep his mind sharp. The magazine also had anagrams and all sorts of brainteasers.

When I was a teenager, I loved to do crosswords and sometimes even competed with my dad, but I was never as dedicated as he was. One day he decided that he was going to complete the hardest crossword that, I would bet, not even Einstein could finish without the help of his wife—because we all know that women are smarter than men. It took my dad a week of consulting several encyclopedias at the library, but eventually he completed the "beast." Right before he penciled in the last letter, all the angels and saints in heaven, including Saint Horizontal Across—the patron saint of the dedicated crossword people—sang, "Hallelujah, bravissimo. All I can say is wow. But if you're going to do it again, make sure to get some help from Google."

In high school, my friend Roberto used to bring crosswords to history class. He had good reason to do so, because the professor was profoundly boring. I sat next to Roberto at the back of the class and would sometimes help him solve the puzzle. One day Roberto got stuck at "three down, four across": a young brother and sister kidnapped by a witch who lived deep in the forest in a house made of candy. He had it on the tip of his tongue but couldn't name it.

Meanwhile, the professor continued his lesson about capitalism and communism. He asked the entire class, "Who were the two philosophers who influenced Karl Marx?" Nobody seemed to have a clue, although we later learned that the answers were Kant and Hegel.

Due to some mysterious coincidence, as the professor repeated the question for the second time, Roberto had a breakthrough—he had the solution to the puzzle. Without thinking, he shouted, "Hansel and Gretel!" I thought that was brilliant. It made sense to me that Hansel and Gretel were the minds behind the Communist Manifesto. Egalitarianism and justice for all, whether you like chocolate or peppermint candy. Join the revolution and you'll get an endless supply of jelly beans and eggnog!

However, the history teacher didn't seem to agree with me and was quite disappointed by Roberto's answer. The entire class was laughing hysterically, although it wasn't the first time chaos had found its way to school. Quite a commotion had occurred the previous week during French class. The teacher was very adept in writing French words on the blackboard. She was a constant reminder of how the French culture had sophistication and class, with so much impeccability and delicacy. *C'est plus facile . . . croissant, crepe, merci beaucoup.* I didn't mind her work, but I wished she would smile a little more. However, to the class's surprise, something would light up that smile on her face during class. It was during a pause between one of her "Rrrrrrrrrrs" and "Ooh la las" that someone in the class let out a big fart. Not just any fart, and not from just anybody. It was an eight-second fart from the most corpulent student in the class. There was a moment of silence, or rather uncertainty, and then the entire class, including the professor, broke into an interminable laugh. One simple fart, and all her French elegance and style vanished.

So, the question arises: What is it about a bodily function that makes us laugh so much and yet be so offensive as well? To add some clarity, the anagram of the word *fart* is *frat*, like a fraternity or brotherhood. Maybe the answer is that we're all brothers and sisters united by farting. This could have also been a good Communist slogan—much more efficient than the one created by Marx and Hegel and their hysterical friend, Lenin. More farts, less stress. Because, as much as people act disgusted by this subject, farting makes us all human. Why is that idiot in North Korea playing with nuclear bombs? Instead, he should spend more time thinking about the precariousness of life and liberating the stomach and intestines of impertinent gases and acids. I was eight years old when I had to learn how to deal with the taboos surrounding this topic.

One summer while vacationing with my family at Forte dei Marmi on the Tyrrhenian Sea, I went with my brother Leonardo to visit our friend, Giacomo. When we arrived at his home, his family and some other people were playing card games in the garden. This was a luxurious house with tall pines all around the property. The breeze coming from the sea was intensified by the tree branches and made for a pleasant afternoon. I sat down at the table with the players, as I liked to watch other people playing cards. I knew most of the rules of the game, Ramino (or Scala 40), but I didn't have enough experience to be part of the match. The strategy of the game is like a crossword puzzle, as the key is to find the missing card. It helps to have a good memory and a dose of luck. In the meantime, my brother was sitting with his friends in the veranda, drinking refreshing cocktails and listening to the latest summer hits.

Suddenly, the muscles of my intestines started contracting and relaxing in an irregular way, and I had to make an effort to stay in control of my stomach. This went on for some time, and the discomfort seemed worse in my mind. Finally, my brother came to tell me that it was time to go back home. I was relieved. I got up from the chair and raised my leg on the chair to tie my shoe. In that moment, I involuntarily let out a big one. It wasn't a big deal, really. We were outside with the wind blowing. Essentially, I didn't offend anybody's nasal passages, but I'd created a moment of discomfort. In that second, my face became red, and the older people looked at me with their jaws dropped.

My heartbeat became irregular, and I had to figure out how to extricate myself from the awkward situation. It couldn't be undone; we couldn't go back in time. I'd farted. It was that simple. Did I have to apologize? Did I have to cover my face? Did I have to laugh? What does an eight-year-old do after releasing gas? I decided to be honest. Where is the dignity unless there's honesty? I'd endured two hours of fighting with my guts. Honestly, I felt better. Therefore, I said, "Ahhhhhhhh, that felt great!" I continued to tie my shoe, ignoring the confused faces who were staring at me. I said goodbye to everybody, and I left with my brother.

On the way home, my brother said, "I understand that you had to let it out, but why did you have to emphasize it?"

I replied, "Well, what was I supposed to do? I was trying to be honest. I held it for two hours." My brother told me that in the future, the best thing to do is conceal the fact as much as possible, negate the evidence with an incongruent gesture, and quickly move away from the scene.

Had I committed a crime? No. But a release of air of this type *can* be offensive. Some circumstances are more forgiving than others. Indeed, museums can be an optimal place to keep a low profile. I know that from personal experience. I was at the Getty Museum in Los Angeles once when I came across a group of people sitting in front of a painting by Bonaventura

Lamberti, known as "Il Bolognese." Then I smelled something. I smelled it again a few rooms down, in front of Van Gogh's lilies. Who did it? Was it the old lady to my left or the man standing by the wall? People do it. Nobody dies, and life goes on. After all, it's just a fart! A tiny, innocent, yet brave fart! Close-minded bigots need to relax! And you, whoever you were at the museum: Bless you! God loves you even more with your imperfections!

This lecture is over. You can go in peace. Do some crosswords and fart as much as you want.

Penguins and Such

Penguins are known for being monogamous. Once they meet their mating partners, they stick with each other for the rest of their lives. It's a nice relationship that I have the privilege to see reflected in my own family as well. My father told me the story of how he courted my mom for months before she finally gave him a kiss. Then he left for the military service, and for eighteen months he wrote her a letter almost every day. My mom and dad weren't allowed to go on a date by themselves. They were always accompanied by relatives of theirs, who functioned as chaperones to make sure that everything was on the up-and-up. There wasn't much room for action or exploration. For my parents, abstinence before marriage was not only a matter of honor; it was also a religious mandate.

My parents married in April 1958; and by January, my sister Gianna was born. They had four more children, including me. When I was little, I thought that they made love only five times, one for each child they had. I wasn't sure what sex was. I was getting puzzling and disparate information, especially on television. I'd heard that sex was pleasurable but that it also carried great responsibility. In fact, every time someone had sex, I thought a child would result; and kids, from my prospective, weren't fun. At church I saw crying and annoying babies, distressed mothers, and absent-minded fathers. How could someone decide to have children? Why had my parents wanted to have kids? Maybe they hadn't wanted to have any, but it just happened as a result of having sex. One day my mom told me that she'd had two miscarriages before I was born. So I figured that my parents hadn't had sex five times, but rather, seven. They had two free bonuses. Lucky them! I'm sure they enjoyed those two extra times more than all the others.

When I was eight, I studied piano for one year, and something happened during that time. Once a week my mom would leave me at my piano teacher's house for an hour. She was a young lady in her early twenties. My first lessons were about *solfeggio* tones. I would sit across the table from my teacher as she instructed me about the rudiments of music and the timing of the notes. Then we started playing the piano. She would wear short skirts, and my eyes would uncontrollably go to her legs while I was trying to keep my hands moving on the keyboard. I didn't have a clue why I was doing it. In my head, I kept reminding myself to pay attention to the keyboard, but my eyes couldn't resist the pleasure of looking at her beautiful thighs. I was exasperated. In addition, I thought I was doing something wrong, as far as religious protocol was concerned, which was so important to my family. I will never know if my teacher realized what was happening. I do know that she kept wearing those skirts and, eventually, I told my mom that I was quitting piano. *Why? Because . . . I don't know, Mom, I just want to quit. Thank you.*

Nudity is normal in Italy. When you go to the beach, seeing topless women is quite the norm, including seeing naked women who one would hope would have the sensitivity to cover themselves and avoid traumatizing adults and children alike. On television, showgirls dance with their curvy bottoms right in front of the camera; and magazines are full of nude women advertising salami and provolone. But what was interesting with the piano teacher was the appeal of her dress, and the fact that what was *not* seen was more exciting than what was. As a young boy, I was simultaneously excited and fearful of the energy emanating from her body. That was my second experience of the unknown taking charge of my senses after having had a similar feeling when I tried Nutella for the first time!

At my elementary school, the most beautiful girl was Patrizia. I'm not sure when boys decide that girls are trophies to aspire to win, but that happened in my fourth-grade class. One day the teacher told me to sit next to Patrizia, and I went into a state of shyness. I couldn't even turn my head toward her. I didn't think I was a good candidate to go on a date with her because I was slightly overweight. My mom was feeding me very well, and I had a chubby face that made me feel uncomfortable around the beauty queen of our class. But I did have a fan, Stefania, who shared some of the same weight insecurities. We held hands during recess, and I was frequently invited to her home to eat cookies and play board games. That must have been my first date ever. But no kissing. Dating was about sharing a cookie.

Middle school didn't give me the opportunity to explore the strange feeling I had when I looked at attractive women. In fact, I went to a boarding school for boys only from age eleven to fourteen. So, I had to wait until I was fourteen to once again enter into the mysterious world of the other gender with the hope of understanding what it was all about. My three years at boarding school were like living in a medieval castle, full of art and books. It provided a very stimulating intellectual perspective, but slowed my social skills, especially with girls. This became apparent when I started high school. Most of the students knew each other from attending middle school at the same institution. I was an outsider, the new kid on the block who'd studied at a boarding school in Rome. Quite unusual. In addition, I appeared shy, although I was good-looking. I could see that the girls were interested in me, but they weren't sure how to approach me. What was I all about?

When I entered a high school for classical study in Florence, I decided to live in a room in the church that my parents attended every Sunday. The church was only fifteen minutes from the school in Florence, while my parents' home was about an hour away. Every morning I would leave the church with my scooter, a Piaggio Vespa 50, and go to school in downtown Florence. I didn't tell my secret to the other students. I wasn't sure if they would have understood. I felt weird about my background at the boarding school and for living in a church. Was I going to be a priest? Even if the idea had crossed my mind when I was in elementary school, I determined that I wasn't one for celibacy. Since I had a strong attraction to the opposite sex, it was going to be difficult to be a Catholic priest. Not impossible, but painful for sure.

One morning during lunch, as I was in line to get a pastry at the cafeteria, I saw her. She had straight blonde hair, blue eyes, and porcelain skin. We looked at each other as if we'd met before. She giggled and whispered to her friend in the hall. It took me a few days to get up the courage to talk to her. Her name was Guinevere, like the lover of Lancelot, the Round Table knight. I think that having some mystery is a good tactic to make women curious and, if one isn't creepy about it, the unknown can be the bait to get the momentum going. Without any effort, the shadow of my impenetrability had its effect. In fact, one day Guinevere invited me to her friend's party. She gave me the address, and I assured her that I was going. That weekend, I didn't go back home but stayed at the church instead. On Saturday night, I told the couple who lived there with me that I was going to see a friend of mine, and that, possibly or rather hopefully, I was going to be late. I put on some cologne, my favorite jacket, jumped on the Vespa 50, and went down to Florence.

As I entered the house party, I saw several people from my school but none of my classmates. The room was dark, with a psychedelic light flashing on the walls of the living room. Guys and girls were talking, laughing, and listening to music.

It was a nice scene. Then, Guinevere came out of the crowd and started talking to me. We danced, but I was clumsy. She smiled. Nothing exciting happened in those few minutes when we danced together. I think she became annoyed by my feeble response to her clear advances. Staying in the moment is crucial. Once the right time has slipped away, it's over with a woman. And it was over soon enough for me. To say that I regret that missed opportunity would not do justice to the person I am now. But I did learn a lesson from that situation: a woman respects a confident man more than anything else. I saw Guinevere again at school, but I soon became the guy who missed his chance to have the school love story of the year.

My first kiss came later, with a girl three years older than I was. That kiss was like knocking on my friend's door before dinner. She'll invite you over, she'll tell you that she's sorry and that she wasn't prepared for your unexpected visit, and she'll say she didn't cook much. You'll look at the table, and to you, it doesn't appear lacking: there's plenty of food there. But then you'll say that you're not too hungry anyhow, and you were just stopping by to say hi. However, she invites you to sit down, you have a little appetizer, and by the end of the night, you've consumed a full dinner. My first kiss started as a timid taste of the appetizers and ended up being a full dinner, including dessert. Basically, the more I ate, the more I *wanted* to eat. My "relationship" with the girl didn't last long, but it gave me a taste of what it means to be a penguin. Let me rephrase: of *becoming* a penguin. I will explain.

The relationship between my mother and father was meant to be like the relationship between two penguins. They were born in an era when there wasn't much room for error; and if there was an error, it wasn't legally dealt with, because divorce was rare, especially for a Catholic family. I know that my parents were lucky to have found each other. When I see them, as they've reached sixty years of marriage, there's no doubt that they're made for each other. They must have had difficult moments, but no relationship is immune from obstacles in life. Their bond is solid, although they both joke about getting a divorce tomorrow. The same can be said about my sisters and brothers, who married young and are still with their significant others. I, on the other hand, went a different route. I had to be a porcupine for a while until I could transform into a penguin. I was the ugly duckling who eventually transformed into a swan. I will get to that later. But before I tell my story, I want to share what my sister told me about the secret of marriage, or better yet, the secret of becoming a perfect penguin.

It was a pleasant late-summer evening. My oldest sister, Gianna, had invited my girlfriend, Viktoria, and me to her home for dinner. When my sister invites me to dinner, I never hesitate to accept. She's a great cook, and even when she makes the simplest dish, it tastes delicious. That night she made polenta, porcini mushroom sauce, green beans with tomato sauce, and pollo cacciatore. Giovanni, my brother-in-law, brought dessert from a local bakery. It was a flat sweetbread made with a special type of fruit called fragolina, or "little strawberry." We also drank a wonderful red wine from Carmignano and a homemade limoncello to finish.

My sister is very inquisitive. Growing up, we didn't have a close relationship because the twelve-year gap between us was rather substantial. When she was in high school, I was still a baby. When she got married, I had just turned nine. Today, our relationship has deepened because age is no longer a significant factor. She's almost sixty (I'm 46), but you'd never be able to tell because she takes very good care of herself. She still has the energy of a twenty-year-old. I could say the same for her husband, Giovanni. Now he's lost most of his hair and has a few wrinkles, but he's in great shape for a sixty-two-year-old.

What's even more incredible is the length of time they've been a couple. The decades that have passed since their marriage have not diminished the love they have for each other. If anything, time has made their bond grow stronger. This is obvious to me, and I've heard numerous stories about their life together. Even a stranger would be able to notice their affection. They often receive compliments for their effortlessness as a couple even when they travel outside of Italy.

That night, while eating dessert and drinking limoncello, I asked Gianna, "What is the secret to a happy marriage?"

Gianna responded without hesitation, "Patience. It's all about patience. It's the indispensable virtue for living together day after day." That's why *patience* in Italian is often followed by the adjective *holy*, as in *santa pazienza* (holy patience). According to Gianna, patience isn't meant to be just positivity or acceptance of everything, but rather the awareness, the understanding, and the calmness required to resolve pressing situations. Patience is the strong foundation that makes a marriage last.

It was such a wise and enlightening conversation, and my sister was so profound. I then asked her husband, Giovanni, "What do *you* think is the secret to a happy marriage?"

He laughed and responded, "Sure, I agree that patience is important. However, the real secret of marriage is much simpler: chemicals. To be more precise: dopamine, serotonin, oxytocin, and endorphins. And how do you get all of them? Very, very simple. Can you guess, or do you want me to give you a hint? I know that you know. Yes, that's it: lots of sex. Good sex is the magic potion that keeps the marriage in check." Gianna rolled her eyes, but I think Giovanni also had a point about the chemical balance in a marriage.

I now had the secret recipe to a lasting relationship: patience and love. Indeed, the secret to a happy marriage is patience in all phases of life, including patience, perseverance, and dedication in bed. And real penguins know that very well!

Porcupines

On the way to finding my penguin soul mate, I had to endure the joys and sorrows of being a porcupine. Why, of the entire animal kingdom, do I see myself as a porcupine? Well, first, a porcupine is friendly. He is also genuinely promiscuous, in that he must go through trials and errors to find his ideal mate. He is also to be admired because he must take some serious risks dealing with the female porcupine, a task to undergo more than just carefully. Any wrong move could be the end of the relationship and result in many "Ouches," "Oopses," and "Ohs."

My porcupine story started when I was eighteen and went out with my friends to a nightclub. Those were the days of my version of *Saturday Night Fever*. My friends Roberto, Claudio, and I were regulars at Panda, a dance club in the countryside of Pistoia, the town right next to my home. The night began with the "ultimate" shower, an endless one that eventually made the entire bathroom and the rest of my house a giant cloud of steam. Then, when the fog had cleared from the bathroom, I shaved the few mustache hairs I had. I proceeded to put on Benetton underwear, Ralph Lauren socks, the gold necklace from my First Communion, and Levi jeans. I put on my black-and-white dotted Versace shirt (one of many in my wardrobe, but one that I could never wear in the States unless I lived in San Francisco's Castro District), followed by the final touch: a pound of gel in my hair that transformed me into the twin brother of John Travolta—or so I hoped. I wore my expensive American Timberland shoes and then sneaked out of the house to avoid my mother's threats that I'd better be back home by midnight. I was off to Roberto's, where I would meet with the rest of the gang.

By the time I arrived at his home, it was 10 p.m., and the night was still young. Entering Roberto's apartment, I had to fight with more fog, because he'd also had a long shower with an overflow of steam. Roberto had put on what smelled like an entire bottle of Gucci perfume, enough that the bouncer at the dancing club already knew he was on his way. Shortly afterward, Claudio was at the door. *"Ci stagguarda?"* was the usual remark in his Neapolitan dialect, meaning: "What are you looking at? Let me in." People from Naples are naturally funny. They don't have to make any effort.

It was now 11 p.m. but still too early to go dancing. Most of the club patrons wouldn't show up until after midnight, so we had plenty of time for a drink before going out. We went to La Maddalena, a pub a few miles from Roberto's house, owned by two gay brothers who were friends of ours. The bar is still in existence today but has changed since the glorious days of our youth. The walls were painted with eloquent quotes about the love life of one of the brothers, Giordano: *your fault; make it up to me; you are bad; kiss me wherever; forever mine; come here, baby; touch me; mon amour; bad boy;* and many more that subtly described his relationships. Giordano was extremely friendly and fun—and very flamboyant. We respected gay people, but our motto was that we liked cherries not bananas. Being gay in Italy, the official headquarters of the Catholic Church, isn't easy. But Roberto and I respected Giordano's lifestyle and appreciated that he wasn't competition for us in the area of love.

I drove a basic Fiat, not the most respectable car to show up with at the club. Therefore, we would park far away in an alley and make up a story about our rich friend who'd given us a ride in his Porsche. We paid our entrance fee and went into the club. We then looked around to evaluate the "women situation" and light up some cigarettes. Marlboro, the cigarette of the cowboy, was the top brand to smoke. However, they were expensive, so we kept an empty pack that we'd fill up with cheaper cigarettes. Sometimes people would ask us for a smoke, but after the first puff, they'd notice that they weren't Marlboros. Seeing their perplexed faces, we'd tell them, "They don't taste exactly like the Marlboros you buy at the store because these were smuggled in directly from America by a friend." That little white lie made us look cool, as if we had connections to the American Mob.

Then it was time for a drink. Getting to the bar was a true obstacle course. But after thirty-eight punches to the gut, we made it up there. The bartender knew us. "Same as always?"

"Yes, thank you, Fabio, extra dry, as usual." It was no wonder that we nicknamed him "The Chemist." All we wanted was to diminish our awareness and feel spaced-out for a few hours.

The most important moment of the night was the thirty minutes of slow songs that gave us an opportunity to dance with the girls. We positioned ourselves next to the columns surrounding the club and targeted the ones we wanted to dance with. It was a long and careful wait. We tried not getting distracted by the girl dancing on the cube, spinning around on her eighteen-inch heels. Finally, the moment we'd been waiting for was announced by the DJ. The lights dimmed, and I walked over to a girl and asked her, "Do you mind dancing?" She agreed, and I could hear myself saying, "Yeah, baby, that $200 Versace shirt was totally worth it!" I led her to the dance floor, and in the middle of the most sentimental song, I kissed her. But as I did so, a reflection from the psychedelic light lit up her face, and I discovered that she wasn't the girl I'd targeted for hours. She wasn't my top choice, and I didn't ask for her number, if that paints a clear enough picture. . . .

After a couple hours, my feet started to hurt. Going to the restroom would be too complicated due to the tightness of my jeans. The slow music finished, and the DJ went back to playing some house music. It was three in the morning when we decided to go back home. As soon as we left the club, we were hit with a blast of cold. To save money, we hadn't brought our coats, to avoid paying a fee. We raced to the car as the cold seeped into our skin. "Start the heat, start the heat!" my friend yelled as soon as we shut the door.

Then we headed to the final part of the outing: getting a fresh pastry from a local bakery. At this time of the night (or technically, morning), the only available food was at the local bakery that was preparing its nightly production to be delivered to the surrounding cafés, which would later be breakfast for the people who were currently sleeping while we were still wandering the streets of Pistoia. As we ate the cream-filled desserts, we knew that the chemical interaction of the alcohol, dough, and cream would be explosive the next day. A long session sitting on the toilet was going to be inevitable after waking up in the early afternoon. But for tonight, we had our moment of glory.

Some nights we would have better luck at the club, meeting some cute girls whom we'd date for a while. Dating was about impressing the girl, especially during the first stages of the relationship. Therefore, when I went to pick up a girl for our first date, I would ask my dad if I could borrow his car. He was always cooperative even though he was very religious. I'm not sure if he understood what was going on or what I was up to, but he might have had some idea. My dad was patient with me, almost as if he was experiencing his youth again through me, although, the "action" in his experience was much more restrictive compared to that of my generation. Maybe he wished he'd lived in my more open era . . . who knows?

If I was really into a girl, I had to choose a good restaurant for our first date, which meant *mucho dinero*. One of my choices was Sabatini in Florence. I called to make a reservation, with the hope that they were full, which would have made my secondary and cheaper choice an honest excuse, but I never got that lucky: they always had a table for me. They would rather cancel the reservation for a Japanese tour group than tell me that all their tables were reserved. Any investment company would have advised me that inviting a girl to Sabatini on the first date is one of the riskiest ventures; even the guy who invented the Ponzi scheme wouldn't have taken that chance. But what does a twenty-year-old know about investing wisely in "love affairs"? That's why I was a porcupine in the first place and not yet a penguin.

Now, many women seem to be perpetually on a diet; however, when they cross the door of an expensive restaurant, they're rarely on any type of calorie restriction.

"Should we get some wine?" I asked my date to be polite, even though I was almost certain that she would just go for San Pellegrino water.

"How about some Brunello di Montalcino? Reserve, of course."

"Are you sure? Wouldn't the wine of the house be a lighter choice?"

"No, no, I love Brunello."

I love Brunello too. It's the price tag that I'm not too crazy about. And when did she become a wine connoisseur all of a sudden?

"Should we order some appetizers?" I asked. There was no need for further suggestions at that point. She was on a roll. She reminded me of one of those empty silos used to ferment pilsner beer, as she was ordering all kind of food: pâté de foie gras, spinach flan with white truffles, turnovers, fettuccine with porcini mushrooms, shrimps and scampi with black truffles, and sliced fillet of steak. Anything else? No, I think we ordered all that was on the menu! And to seal the end of the food parade, let's not forget liqueur, espresso, and grappa. Then, but only then, was it time to pay the bill.

"Sweetheart, I'm going to pay," to which she replied, "Oh, please," but she hadn't even tried to offer to help.

The hostess looked at my credit card and asked, "Is this the only card you have?" As she slid the card through, it felt as if I was donating plasma at the blood bank. I would need to ask my brother to work for a month at his bakery, delivering bread at four in the morning, to cover the dinner bill.

We left the restaurant, and I was almost flying. My wallet felt so much lighter leaving than when I'd arrived. Hand in hand, we strolled down the streets of Florence toward the movie theater Oden in Strozzi Square.

"How about we see *Rocky III*? Did you see the previous one?" I asked her.

"No, no, *Rocky*, please," she responded.

"What else is out there?" I asked.

"*Even Maria Gets the Blues*."

"Is that a movie, or gossip you want to share about your friend Maria?"

"No, it's a movie. Just released. It should be fun."

"I can't wait to see Maria's blues."

The movie made me very sleepy. Before I dropped her off, she wished me a good night and left me with a kiss. Would this kiss be the key to her heart? How could I know? In retrospect, I now know that my journey toward becoming a penguin would be a long one. I had to endure more dinners, more sappy romantic comedies, and more porcupine adventures before I would find the lasting love of the monogamous penguins. Never say never! Not even a bachelor such as George Clooney could escape his destiny, and look at him today: one of the most irreducible porcupines transformed into a penguin that can be found walking around his villa on Lake Como with his wife and twins. It's only a matter of time. . . .

Porcupines

Nutella

C= mc² or Energy = milk and double chocolate. That's the secret formula of the universe, the one thing that can unite us all. Einstein was the scientist behind the discovery of the universal formula, but the story of chocolate and what would become a famous spread goes far back in time. It began in an unknown forest on the shores of Hazelnut Beach.

Once upon a time in America, there lived a tribe of people, the descendants of the Wonka family. The chief of the tribe was Standing Toblerone, who had a daughter by the name of Chocohontas. The tribe lived peacefully in the tropical forest—hunting, gathering, and making a delicious mix from sugar, chocolate, and hazelnuts. One day the chief gathered the members of the tribe together and told them, "I called this tribal meeting for two reasons. First, we need to do a better job of summoning the rain because our crops are drying up. Second, I have a simple but important question for all of you: Who stole the chocolate spread from the warehouse?" The members of the tribe were stunned that twenty-eight pounds of chocolate spread had disappeared.

Then, Medicine Man spoke. "Wow. Big Chief seems annoyed. But I have a solution. Medicine Man is friendly with Foxy Nose, the great detective from Louisiana Yard. I will call him to investigate." The chief agreed to call off the meeting. Medicine Man went to the top of the mountain and made some smoke signals to call the detective.

From the other side of the valley, Foxy Nose responded to the smoke signal. "What's so funny?" asked the surprised detective. And the smoke conversation continued.

"Nothing's funny," responded Medicine Man.

"Why, then, did you send me the LOL signal?" replied the detective from the other side.

"Sorry, I meant SOS," said Medicine Man, realizing his mistake.

"What's the emergency?" Foxy Nose asked.

"Big Chief needs your help. All the chocolate spread has disappeared. Somebody must've stolen it."

"No worries. This is the perfect job for my sensitive muzzle. I will be over in a minute."

While the detective was examining the evidence, one of the members of the tribe, Heavy Balls, went to the chief's teepee. "Chief, your daughter, Chocohontas, has been missing for the last few days. I'm not saying that she's responsible for the missing chocolate spread, but she may know something."

"Heavy Balls, I know you like Chocohontas, so don't start throwing around accusations. What do you mean she's gone? Did you follow her into the forest?"

"Chief, if you let me, I will follow her and find out."

"Yes, Heavy Balls, please keep an eye on her, and let us know what you find, including our detective, Foxy Nose."

Heavy Balls didn't have to research any further. He'd already followed Chocohontas into the forest for several days and saw her with a stranger, a white man. Heavy Balls was furious because he liked Chocohontas and was hoping to marry her one day. Heavy Balls reported his findings to the chief. Standing Toblerone was outraged. He ordered a group of men to capture the white man, who was brought to the chief's knees. Chocohontas begged her father to release the unknown man.

"Who are you?" Standing Toblerone asked.

"I am Luigi Pulcinella."

"Why are you here?"

"I escaped my Italian mom, the meanest mother on Earth. In my house, she hides all the gummy bears and jelly beans and shows no mercy when I beg her for some Tootsie Rolls. When I was little, she spanked me with my hand still in the bowl of candy. She told me that she couldn't afford to send me to the dentist one more time. I got tired of my growling stomach and sailed the world to find some candy in the land of plenty."

"I see that you *did* find some candy. In fact, *you* are responsible for stealing the jars of spread in our warehouse, and for this reason, you are sentenced to die."

Chocahontas ran in front of her father, pleading, "If you kill him, you will have to kill me too. Don't you see that he's just a simple Italian guy with a sweet tooth, in search of some candy due to his cruel, uncompromising mother? He didn't steal the spread. I was with him. He only had some strawberry jam, which I made for him, but that's all, I promise. He's not what you think. I love him very much."

At that moment, the detective Foxy Nose noticed something about the chief's father, Pecan Pie. "Excuse me, Grandpa Pecan Pie, could you please show us your finger? It may offer us some clue of what has really happened here. Your finger is brown, isn't it? That's the unmistakable sign of dipping into the spread. It was you, wasn't it? You probably know where the jar is hidden."

"It's not what you think, but I confess: I stole the jar," said Pecan Pie.

"Father, you did this?" asked Standing Toblerone, looking surprised and mortified as his father admitted to committing a criminal act punishable by listening to the song "Macarena" for eight hours.

"Yes, but I had no choice. Your mother forced me to do a blood test, and my cholesterol level was too high. So, she has forbidden me to have any spread, not even a little taste, and after a while I couldn't take it anymore. I stole the jar, the only way I could dip my finger in the chocolate spread without your mother finding out."

From the teepee emerged the chief's mother, Almond Joy, who ran toward Pecan Pie with a slipper in her hand. "I can't believe it. Especially after what Medicine Man said about the cholesterol and triglyceride levels in your blood. Why don't you listen? You can't have any chocolate spread until you lose some weight and get back in shape. You can't even get on your horse without help!"

The jar was found in an abandoned hut in the forest, where Pecan Pie had dragged it to eat without being bothered. The jar was open but still half-full. It was brought back to the warehouse, much to the joy of Standing Toblerone and the reassurance of Almond Joy, who also loved the spread as much as she liked to prohibit its consumption by her poor husband. She was right: a single spoon of the spread had many calories because it was made with whole milk, as the fat-free version hadn't been invented yet—and frankly, didn't taste as good.

Finally, everything was resolved. Pecan Pie was forgiven. He only had to write: "My wife is always right" three hundred times, which was painful, but better than listening to the "Macarena" song. In addition, Standing Toblerone had to come to terms with Chocohontas being in love with Luigi—but they were so cute together!

Obviously, Pecan Pie was prohibited from eating any more spread—at least not until his blood tests showed signs of improvement. Almond Joy kept him under watch at all times, but one day when she was watching *Seven Brides for Seven Brothers* on HBO, Pecan Pie called Luigi and whispered, "Luigi, you're a good guy. You had a hard time with your mom, and I have the same problem with Almond Joy. She is so tough. I need some chocolate spread. At least a spoonful . . . please, help me. But no tell her, okay?"

"Nutella?"

"No tell her. She is going to get mad at me otherwise."

"Ah, Nutella, that's what you call it. The spread? Nutella?"

"No tell her. She hid the key of the warehouse, but I found it. Let's go. But, please, please, "No tell her."

"Nutella . . . the spread Nutella. I like Nutella. Although, Chocohontas's strawberry jam is even better."

After this interaction, the spread came to be known as Nutella, which basically means: *Mind your own business when it comes to chocolate.* So, "No tell her"—don't confess any of your Nutella sins, not even to a priest. What is done is done, and nobody has caused any harm by eating Nutella other than suffering the consequence of eating more than a pound of it, which may leave one's pants a little tighter than usual.

One day when everybody was smoking the pipe around the totem, an eagle dropped a written message. It was from Luigi's mom. She was worried about him and regretted restricting her son so severely. She loved him so much and wanted to know where he was. Luigi was so in love with Chocohantas and was going to marry her. He'd even made peace with Heavy Balls, who consoled himself with another girl, Big Coconut, who was big in every sense. Luigi said to Chocohontas: "I will go get my mother and bring her here to live with us. She will make some great lasagna and margherita pizza for the entire tribe. We will live a happy life in the land of plenty, with much Nutella, tiramisu, *primo* and *secondo*."

The next day, Luigi departed from Hazelnut Beach to get his mom. The canoe was kind of bright and caught the attention of a big fish not too long after Luigi entered the water. The fish in question was none other than Moby Dick, the giant whale who'd caused so much turmoil in the ocean. A few weeks earlier, he'd sunk two ships, the McDonald (also known as the Ark with the double Arch), and the Pint (also known as 16 Ounce). Luigi was eaten in one giant bite by Moby Dick, who then closed his mouth for the rest of the day. Luigi was trapped in the stomach of the whale, but luckily it couldn't digest him. Moby Dick was full of Big Macs and Budweiser from the cargos that it had swallowed previously.

While Luigi was strategizing his way out of the big fish, Moby Dick was swimming back and forth in the ocean to get ready for the marathon of the sea, from New York to Gibraltar. This was an annual race that was going to crown the fastest fish in the world. When Moby Dick got close to Spain, Luigi tickled his throat, and eventually Moby Dick let out a big sneeze that catapulted Luigi onto the beach of Ibiza in the middle of a rave party. Among the crowd, there was a guy, Italian like he was.

Luigi asked him for directions. "Excuse me, how do I get to Milan?"

"Who do you think you're talking to? Do you know who I am? I'm Christopher Columbus."

"I am Luigi Pulcinella. Nice to meet you. Are you Columbus, the one who makes salami and bologna?"

"I am Columbus the famous navigator. I am on my way to discover Nutella. I will bring it to Queen Isabella, who said it will make me famous, rich, and buy me a new villa."

"How do you know about Nutella?"

"The Russian spies told us."

"Bloody Russian spies. They must have intercepted my radio waves when I was listening to the Italian Premier Soccer League lying under the sun on Hazelnut Beach."

Luigi brought his mom to America, where they arrived before Columbus. Luigi told Standing Toblerone of the impending danger of Columbus in search of the Indians.

"Wait a second," said Standing Toblerone. "Indians who?"

Luigi said, "Never mind, it's a long story, but Columbus keeps insisting that you guys are Indians rather than Native Americans. We don't even want to waste our time trying to convince him otherwise. He thinks that the Indians have invented Nutella, and he's coming to steal it for the king of Spain, who wants to rename it

Choco Gordita, which is better than Zorrotella or Churrotella, but still . . . we need to get out of here for the sake of the tribe and the Nutella."

Luigi made sure that any evidence of Nutella was hidden. Standing Toblerone moved to California. Many years later, at the Hotel California, there was an Italian man by the name of Pietro Ferrero, who was vacationing in California. He was following the trail of his ancestor Luigi Pulcinella and found an old piece of paper, which was the Nutella recipe written by Standing Toblerone. Pietro Ferrero went back to Italy and began mass-producing Nutella for the joy of all the people.

This is the true story of how the Nutella spread came to be, although, many mysteries remain. The history books refrain from making official claims about the real story of Nutella because every day somebody comes along with new findings. According to the latest claim, Nutella was invented in ancient Rome by Julio Cesar Chocolatarum, and it is for this reason that Hannibal invaded Italy: to get the Nutella. Nutella was smuggled out of Rome and ended up in the hands of the Vikings, who then took it with them on a trip to North America. Immersed in fog, they lost the five-kilogram jar in Greenland, which was found by the Indians; and the rest, as we know, was done by Standing Toblerone.

But whether this really happened is no longer relevant. What matters is that Nutella exists; therefore, *ergo sum*—we are. Nutella is the answer, and who cares, really, about the question? Do you feel stuck in your life? Don't worry; you can always open a jar of Nutella, because it's there to remind you that there's always sweetness in the world.

Indeed, it was hard growing up with Nutella hidden in the pantry. My mom didn't trust any of us. How could she? Luckily, when I was a little kid, I was smart enough to find the key to open it. And if you don't mind, let's make a deal. If you "no tell her," meaning that you don't tell my mom, I "no tell her," meaning I won't tell yours!

What Do You Mean?

I studied English for five years at school. British English. Then I came to America. And words that I worked so hard to memorize were no longer of use in the United States. What happened to *hoover, lift, loo, motorway,* and *queue*? American English isn't completely different, but it sounds rather informal compared to the Oxford vernacular. I found myself perplexed by this new lingo, trying to figure out what people around me were talking about. In my mind, I was shouting, *"Che cazz'dice,"* which is Italian slang for "What the heck are you saying?"

To learn a new language as an adult isn't easy. I'm not trying to make excuses, but the best time to learn anything is when you're little, with a full capacity of brain cells. Scientists would agree with me. However, life is also a never-ending learning experience. It just so happened that my real English lessons happened later in life when I moved to America at the age of twenty-six.

Luckily, as an Italian, I had a few tricks to help me survive in the chaos of a new country. Italians are well known for gesturing. We've become experts out of necessity. Historically, Italy has seen various waves of people speaking different languages. *Sprechen Sie Deutsch? Parlez-vous français? Cómo estás mi amigo?* What about this: *Nǐ shì wǒ de péng yǒu ma?* Is it Chinese or Korean? Italians couldn't keep up with everybody; therefore, they decided to use their body language to deal with foreigners. Taking into consideration that Italian has many dialects, there are countless variations of the same gesture depending on where you live. Italians may not know a single word of the language being spoken but will find a way, utilizing their arms, hands, legs, and faces. The act of expressing oneself with gestures may not be elegant, but it gets results.

Another difficult stage in this process is translating verbatim from one language to another. Even if the translation is grammatically correct, that doesn't mean it makes sense in English. This is especially true with idiomatic phrases. One day I was watching a football match with some friends. The quarterback was tackled at the ten-yard line and fumbled the ball, which got picked up by the other team.

"Come on, what's he doing?" my friend yelled.

Then I shouted from the back of the room, "He makes the chickens laugh!"

"What? What chickens? There are no chickens," replied my friend.

"I'm saying he's not good. He makes the chickens laugh," I explained. My friend was positive that he'd never seen a chicken laugh. But this is an Italian expression used when someone does something stupid. Chickens aren't smart animals. So, if they see you acting in a way they can reasonably determine to be stupid, then what they saw must have been really stupid. Therefore, the quarterback's play was ridiculed by the chickens, who thought they could have done better.

After the game, we planned a tailgate party the following weekend at the Chargers stadium in San Diego. "Who's going? Is Keenan going to be there?" some of the people asked.

I responded, "Keenan will be there. I know my chickens." Chickens again?

My friend pointed out to me, "Seriously, what's with you and chickens? First they laugh, and now they're your friends?"

I must admit that chickens are a large component of the Italian repertoire, but the use of chickens in the US is different. In the old days, a farmer knew every animal in the barn by name. He knew every chicken as well, from the roosters to the little chicks. He was also familiar with their personalities. Therefore, the expression "I know my chickens" means knowing people so well that you can predict their actions.

"Okay, man, chickens have a lot to say in Italian. All this chicken talk has made me tired. I'm going home," said my friend.

"Already? It's only nine," I told him.

"Well, I have to wake up early tomorrow morning," he replied.

"Oh, well, I guess you're an early bird, like a chicken!" I exclaimed. But in English, one wakes up with the roosters, as opposed to the Italian saying of going to bed at the same time as the chickens. My friend left. Seriously, he didn't want to hear that word one more time.

Keenan did come to the tailgate party, and I could have said I knew him just like my pockets, which is another expression to indicate that a guy knows someone just as well as what's in the pockets of his pants.

Eventually, people learning a new language will expand their vocabularies. But they may get confused with words that sound similar or with those that have multiple uses and meanings. Two words that sound very alike but have two different meanings are *kitchen* and *chicken*—just in case I haven't discussed this topic enough. One morning I was walking through the hallway of the company I was temping for, and one of the employees greeted me.

"Good morning. How are you doing?" he asked in an energetic voice.

"I feel tired," I said unenthusiastically.

"What happened?" he asked.

"Well, I couldn't sleep. I looked at the clock, and it was five. So I decided to go in the chicken."

He froze for a second. "The chicken?" he inquired.

"Yes," I replied. "I do every morning, don't you?"

"Oh . . . yes . . . sure . . . okay," he stammered.

I continued. "I went in the chicken and had a coffee. Then I felt better. Let's get going here, I have lots to deal with today." It takes some practice, but then one day it clicks, and you realize why people are looking at you weirdly.

Another word that's used in many different contexts is *take*. You can take something from one place to another. You can also take a bus or taxi, or take some time off. Overall, it's about grabbing something and doing something with it. The word *take* came in handy when I first moved to Springfield, Missouri, where I did several odd jobs, including working for a construction company. The job kept me quite busy. My main task was to move supplies around the construction site. I took boxes from one end to the other. I took paint cans and brought them to the walls that were ready for their first coats. I took plaster and wood panels to the appropriate sections of the site. I was running around nonstop because I wanted to show the crew that I was a hard worker.

One day the manager of the construction site called me over and said, "I'm very happy with your work. I always see you hustling. You just moved from Italy, didn't you? I'm not sure what your future holds, but I know that you have the work ethic to succeed wherever you decide to apply your skills."

I was thankful for his encouragement. Sometimes it only "takes" a few words to make somebody's day brighter. The next day I was assigned to a new supervisor. I followed him everywhere and helped with the different tasks we were assigned. After a few hours, he looked at me and said, "I'm going to take a leak." In my brain the word *take* started flashing again. *Take* was an important word. There was a lot of taking to be done, all the time.

I replied, "Do you need any help?" Obviously, he needed help, I thought. I didn't know what *leak* meant in this context, but it had to be heavy, just like the other supplies around the workplace.

He looked stunned, and his face got red. He stammered, "No . . . no . . . you stay here. I don't need any help."

I continued, "Are you sure?"

"I'm positive," he said, and abruptly left.

I was confused. Here I was, willing to help, and he'd refused my assistance in accomplishing this task. I thought that he'd better not gripe about his back or getting a hernia from all that heavy lifting, then. Instead, when he came back, he looked at me very suspiciously and continued to do so for the rest of the day.

Of course, now I know what "take a leak" means. I can't believe how insidious English can be at times. This expression doesn't really make any sense. "Taking a leak" means "to pee"? But that's the fun part about learning how to communicate with each other.

Here I am complaining about English, when Italian is not as straightforward, either. For example, "Spit the frog" (*sputa il rospo*) is an Italian expression used to force somebody to tell the truth. The order comes with the total awareness that the truth may be unsavory, resembling the slimyness of a toad, but that it's better for both parties to let it out rather than stagnate in the pothole. Some people, on the other hand, don't need any invitation to "spit the frog." Nothing will stop them from speaking the brutal truth. In their opinion, it's a waste of time to, as they say in America, "cry over spilled milk." What's done is done. No regrets!

Sometimes we must make choices. For example, what's better, a full bottle of wine or a drunken wife? What's the advantage of having a drunken wife? She's happy and doesn't nag or take her stress out on her husband. If we want the wife drunk, we must give away the bottle of wine. In fact, it's the wife who's going to drink it. Therefore, the Italian expression "You cannot have the bottle of wine and a drunk wife" corresponds to the English saying "You can't have your cake and eat it too."

"Not all doughnuts come out with a hole" is another Italian expression used to help us remember that life doesn't always unfold as we wish. Sure, we might expect the pastry shop to make all doughnuts with a hole, but sometimes it doesn't work out. Things don't always turn out as planned. But hey, enjoy your doughnuts, anyway.

It shouldn't come as a surprise that many Italian expressions involve food. "Good as bread" is used to describe a person who's calm and altruistic. On the other hand, "reheated cabbage" is a phrase that speaks to the attempts to revive a failed relationship. If it didn't work at first, it probably won't work the second time around. However, as much as you warn people, they may not listen to you anyhow. Sooner or later, they'll come back crying and complaining, to which one can ask, "Did you want the bike? Now you've got to ride it," meaning "I told you so."

A fruit that gets a lot attention is the fig, particularly because of its sweetness. Among young people, to "be a fig" (*sei un figo*) means to be a skilled, astute person who's admired for his or her talent or beauty. *"Che figata!"* which is translated as "So cool!" literally means "What a fig!" On the other hand, saying that "you are worth less than a dried fig" is translated as "you are not worth a damn."

An Italian song by Italian comedian Pippo Franco goes like this: "But how cool (fig) is that guy. Look at that shirt and jeans he wears! I like a guy like him. He's a cool guy (fig), but really cool (fig)." As the Swedish pop band Roxette would say, "You got the look," and we would gladly add, the look of a fig!

The banana is also a comedic part of everyday language in Italy because of its shape. It represents a phallic symbol even though I don't know what man would wish it to be yellow and speckled. *Knock, knock! Who's there? Banana. Banana who? The banana that likes to make the chickens laugh. But before I do so, I'm going to take a leak. I'll be right back!*

The Lion and the Gazelle

🦪

*g*rowing up, I wasn't aware of my parents' brilliance. When I was in school, the common nickname for parents was *matusa*, which was short for Methuselah, a legendary biblical character who lived 969 years. The reason we called our parents *matusa* was to stress the fact that they were of another generation, old people who couldn't understand the trials and tribulations of us poor teenagers who were dealing with a variety of issues, from difficult girlfriends and boyfriends to mean professors. Basically, parents were a different species. Not to mention all the rules we had to obey. It was nonsense that we had to be back home by 2 a.m. Didn't they realize that the real fun at clubs starts then? Our spoiled life was so difficult, and our parents were so cruel! Eventually, we become adults and realize that it was thanks to our parents' wisdom that we lived past our teenage years and came out in one piece.

My parents didn't have much schooling. They were small children during World War II, and with the victory of the Allied forces, the Italian government was more concerned with reconstruction efforts than properly educating its youth. The only requirement was the completion of elementary school, which meant that most children started working as early as ten years old. My father was lucky enough to complete eighth grade. My parents had to learn on their own to compensate for their lack of education and matured swiftly in the process of contributing to their families' finances. Both of my parents had to stay curious and learn on their own to both survive and to appreciate what they had.

One day my father told me the fable of the lion and the gazelle. Every morning, somewhere in Africa, a lion wakes up and knows that he must run to catch his lunch. The same morning, not too far away from the lion, a gazelle wakes up, and he knows that he must run to escape from the grip of the lion's mouth. Therefore, in life, it's not worth the time to figure out if we're lions or gazelles. What matters is to run! My father didn't have to elaborate further, as my mom was a living example that with five children, she didn't have time to figure out which side of the fence she was on. She had to run too. My parents may have been *matusa*, but they taught me many things. In fact, the story of the lion and the gazelle was the fundamental lesson that guided me when I moved to the United States.

The American jungle doesn't allow for a great margin of failure. Or better yet, people can fail, but they better stand back up before anyone important notices. After several jobs, including delivering newspapers, mowing golf courses, working for restaurants, and toiling in several factories, I felt confident enough with my English to make use of my accounting studies. I first worked part-time for two different businesses as an accounting assistant, learning the rudimentary skills of accounting in English as well as how to use Microsoft Excel and Word. I had previously completed my accounting studies using double-entry notebooks instead of software programs. Then, in 2002, I made the big step of applying for a real job with a public company. The job they'd advertised was for a corporate accountant to work closely with the vice president of Finance. The first week of January, I received a call to present myself at a specific time and day at the company's headquarters.

It was just a matter of going for it, and I knew that I could get the job if I instilled in myself the confidence of the lion or gazelle. On the morning of the interview, I put on my suit and looked myself in the mirror. "You got this," I told the face looking back at me. I drove for an hour to a town I didn't even know existed in San Diego County. I got out of the car, took a deep breath, and walked confidently toward the building.

"Good afternoon, how may I help you?" asked the receptionist at the front desk.

"Hello, I'm here to see Mike for the corporate accountant position."

"Sure. I'll inform him that you're here. Your name?"

"Samuele Bagnai," I responded.

"Thank you. Please take a seat. Can I get you a glass of water?"

"Sure, thank you."

I sat down and grabbed the only reading material available on the table in front of me. It was the company's annual report. I would have preferred to continue reading my interview-preparation books, *Sweaty Palms* or *Knock 'em Dead*. Anything was better than numbers in that moment, but I needed to keep my nervous mind busy. I'm glad I did, because reading the annual report in those fifteen minutes was one of the determining factors of my hiring.

Job interviews in America require a lot of preparation. It took hours to rehearse my answers to the questions suggested in the training books. In comparison, my last job interview in Italy didn't require so much time and effort. In fact, the process only took a few minutes. Giovanni, my previous employer, only asked me, "Who sent you?" and I replied, "Giuseppe Barba Gelata." And with that, I was hired.

Finally, the receptionist called my name. She walked me to the meeting room, and there stood Mike with his white shirt, dark tie, and a welcoming attitude, although I could sense he was slightly uncomfortable, or maybe tired?

"Nice to meet you. My name's Mike. I'm the vice president of Finance."

"Good morning, Mike."

"You mean, good afternoon."

"Right, afternoon."

"I wish it was still morning. Today is flying by, and I still have so much to do. We're overworked and understaffed. This is the busiest time of the year, with so many new SEC requirements, not to mention nonstop auditor requests."

"I can imagine," I said.

Mike looked at me inquisitively. I knew I'd gotten his attention with my accent. Well, now that I was here, I was going to play all my cards. I'd remembered to wear my *cornicello*, an Italian amulet shaped as a little horn, to protect against the "evil eye" (or *malocchio*) and bad luck in general. I knew I had to make this interview worthwhile, and I figured that anything and everything would help. I mentally did the sign of the cross "in the name of the Father, the Son, and the Holy Spirit," and included the Holy Mother too, just in case.

"Sit down, please." Mike said. "Tell me about yourself."

I'd gone through so many job interviews by that point, with the same mundane questions and predictable answers.

You want me to tell you something about myself? How cool would it be if I could say what I really wanted, starting from the unequivocal fact that I'm Italian. That way we can avoid any misunderstandings about my accent. As you can see, I'm already gesturing with my hands. And it's fine if you couldn't guess my nationality because the stereotypical Italian is short, loud, and chronically late. What can I say? I've been in this country long enough to understand that punctuality is key. I wish we could have done this job interview at my dinner table—the experience would have been completely different. I was thinking, since we're going to be here a while, talking about my skills and how I would be a great fit for your organization, why don't we have a cappuccino and maybe a cigarette? Go ahead and order a couple of cannoli. By the way, how do you like my suit? I bought it for my sister's wedding, and it still fits pretty good, doesn't it? We can go over the wedding-party details some other time, but I can guarantee it was wild. . . .

"Tell me about your work experience," Mike said.

The CEO of my previous company was Lucky Luciano . . . just kidding. I've never been a member of the Mob, if that's what you were thinking.

"Why do you want to work for our company?"

Well, my current boss is kind of a jerk. He's very demanding and doesn't seem to have a life outside of work. He gave me a project around closing time that I thought could have waited until the next day. I told him, "Hey, why do this today when it's not urgent? What's the point? Tomorrow is another day!" And I went on to explain that life is short, and we should take time for ourselves outside of work. But he wouldn't listen. It was a difficult situation. I was complaining to my demanding boss, but I knew that if the work didn't get done, there wouldn't be a tomorrow.

"What is your weakness?" Mike asked.

I'm not sure if it's a weakness, but I like women. It's not what you think. Not in that sense. I like women because they're the most beautiful and intelligent beings in the universe. I can't say enough about them. For an Italian man, worshipping a woman is part of his DNA. I have the highest respect for women. Do you know that Dante, Petrarch, and Boccaccio, the most important writers in Italian literature, all used women as their muses and inspirations and considered them the purpose of their existence? But here, with HR . . . I wouldn't want to say something too controversial.

"What are your strengths?"

I make a mean pasta. I can bring the entire office lunch tomorrow. But, please, don't ask me to make pasta Alfredo, which did not originate in Italy. Anything else, just not pasta Alfredo. I would rather make pasta puttanesca. How does that sound? Tomorrow, we'll gather in this room and share a meal with the rest of the employees. Who needs team-building workshops anymore? Pasta is the secret to a successful company.

"Where do you see yourself in five years?"

I don't want you to think that I don't value this job, but my dream is to win the Powerball lottery and move to Fiji.

"What are your salary expectations?"

For that, I would refer to my uncle, Vincenzo Joe Poliziano. He's a very reasonable business owner from Sicily. Try to be courteous and generous with him. His business is in cement shoe production for the Mafiosos.

My interview didn't go exactly in that way, but wouldn't it have been refreshing if I'd had the courage to say what I was truly thinking? Instead, as I was spinning weird thoughts in my head, I had to find the right answers to get the job. I needed it! Now, I laugh at the level of stress I was feeling during that interview, but back then, I felt like I was in a psychological game with my interviewer. Years later, I looked through the glass window of the meeting room to see the latest victim, looking around frantically like a fish out of water. Personally, I wouldn't conduct interviews like that. Let the interviewee relax! Give him or her a drink. Maybe a gin and tonic?

My real interview, not the one in my head, seemed to go well. I could sense that the interviewer liked me. My accent could have been a disadvantage, but I was giving clear and concise answers. Then Mike said, "You live rather far from the office, which could be an issue in the long run." No kidding. I was living hours away. How was I going to pull this off?

It was then, when I thought all hope was lost, that I put all my cards on the table. "I agree," I responded. "As a matter of fact, I'm moving here today."

"What do you mean?" Mike asked.

"When I get out of the interview, I'm going to find an apartment here."

"Wow. We haven't decided our hire for this position yet, and I don't want you to move here, only to be rejected."

"I'll call you tomorrow with my new address. I want to show you how interested I am in this position. I will take the risk."

"Well, you're quite brave in your convictions, but I have another interview right after you. Thank you for coming. I'll stay in touch," he told me.

"I look forward to your call. You'll have my new address tomorrow, I promise."

"Thank you. Have a good rest of the day."

"Goodbye." And I walked out of the meeting room.

I passed the receptionist, thanked her again for the glass of water, and left the building, going out into the afternoon sun. I later found out that the receptionist had told Mike that I was the only interviewee to read the annual report before the interview. Never underestimate a receptionist! While I was walking to my car, I thought, *Now, what?* I'd made a commitment. It really wasn't such a crazy idea, because my current living situation wasn't great, and I had already considered relocating. However, I had to make a decision quicker than expected. I only had a few hours. I couldn't go back into that building and rephrase what I'd just said. I was going to find a home in this town, a place I'd only seen for the first time that day.

I didn't have a cell phone, which would have been useful during that stressful time. I visited three apartment complexes, but they were all overpriced, and the salary of the job I interviewed for wouldn't even cover the rent. I was getting frustrated and discouraged. It was 4 p.m., and I still hadn't completed what I thought was going to be a pretty easy task. I drove to another apartment complex. Not only was the place expensive, but there was no availability. I asked the lease representative if he could help me. He was a young, energetic guy. He asked, "Where are you from?" I found that my accent was a great way to make friends, a sort of icebreaker. We started talking. I didn't go all the way back to when my mom almost gave birth to me on the way to the hospital, but I gave him a little recap of my life. He seemed interested in everything that was outside the norm of this little town. He searched the database and told me that there was a one-bedroom apartment for rent on the other side of the highway—not the greatest part of town, but in a better price range. I thanked him and then started on my way to Vale Terrace Drive.

As I drove, the nice mowed lawns, parks, and flowers faded away, and it became obvious to me why the other side of town was so cheap. I reached the gate where an old gentleman in his seventies came to greet me. I told him I was looking to rent the one-bedroom apartment that he'd listed on the Web. We walked past the community pool, to the end of one of the four structures surrounding the parking lot. The apartment was spacious, private, and quiet. It didn't have the finest carpet, and I could tell that it was an old building, but it would do for now. Besides, I was running out of time. Bill and I went back to the office, where I signed various documents. I shook the landlord's hand and thanked him for helping me on such short notice. Now I had an address to deliver to my potential boss. I knew that this would show Mike that I was serious.

I *did* get a callback from the company. For my second interview, I was going to meet the director of the office branch. When she saw me, she greeted me with a smile.

"Nice to meet you, Sam. My name is Laurie."

"Thank you for giving me the opportunity to interview a second time," I replied.

"So you're from Florence?"

What was I going to say? Yes or no? This hadn't come up in my first interview. Of course I was from Florence, but I thought that maybe I shouldn't divulge too much information. What did these people think about Italians anyhow? Italian people aren't known for being smart with finances. We're better off painting and making sculptures, although I could have mentioned that as a Florentine, I lived near the house where Luca Pacioli had developed the first system of double-entry bookkeeping used by merchants in his *Summa de Arithmetica, Geometria, Proportioni et Proportionalita*. But that might have been too complicated to explain. . . .

"Yes, I'm from Florence."

"Oh my gosh. That's my favorite city in Europe. I love Florence. I could retire there."

What a relief! She loved Florence. It turned out that she'd spent her last semester of college in Europe and had traveled primarily in Italy. For most of the hour, we talked about art and food. We'd nearly forgotten that I was there for a job in finance—not to replace a chef or museum curator. All I wanted was to get this job. I would do anything. Given Laurie's affinity for Italy, I would go so far as to make her tiramisu or bring in a papier-maché copy of the David and put it at the entrance to welcome investors and visitors to the company. But I stood by what I said earlier: I would not make pasta Alfredo.

The interview went well. Laurie told me that it was down to two candidates. I really thought I had the position, after our long conversation about Florence and my recent relocation. Maybe they just didn't want to offer the job to someone too soon. They told me they were going to call a couple of the references I'd included with my résumé.

I went back home. I was restless and couldn't sleep the entire night. My room was surrounded by boxes, as I was moving into the new apartment in a few days. I looked at the red *cornicello*, my lucky-charm necklace. Was it going to bring me luck this time?

The call came. Laurie told me I would be starting that Monday. Thank you, Lord! And thank you, *cornicello*! I'd done it—I'd gotten my first serious job. I also had my own apartment. I was on a roll. Believing had made me accomplish another milestone in my adventure in California. But, whether you find refuge from a lion or you catch the gazelle, the subsequent relief is momentary. Soon enough the obstacles will reappear, and it will be time to run again.

I had slightly embellished my work experience on my résumé, but I knew that my work ethic would make up the difference. Both references had spoken highly about my professional demeanor and skills. When I didn't understand a concept or procedure, I would leave the task incomplete at night and promise that I would finish it by the next morning. After work, I would go to the library and spend hours studying books on finance or accounting until I was sure how to complete the project. Now, this is all second nature to me.

What would I have done without that little story that my dad had told me when I was in Italy? Every morning a lion and a gazelle wake up: it doesn't matter on which side of the fence I stand—I had to run. Indeed. I sometimes run in the role of a gazelle and other times as a lion. I would have never survived the "Go and get it" environment of the American workplace without this story in my back pocket. California isn't as tough as New York; however, the job hunt was more challenging than anything I'd experienced in Italy, where my job interview was based on who I knew, rather than my skills and capabilities.

Cupid

Who is Cupid? How did he get here? But most important: who ordered him? Cupid isn't a latte macchiato that you get at Starbucks. You can't order him on Amazon. It doesn't work that way with Cupid. He comes and goes at his will. What we know for sure is that he comes, sooner or later; and when he does, you're sure to notice.

Cupid is the God of Desire, Attraction, and Affection. He's the son of Venus, the Goddess of Love. Imagine Cupid going to work on a Friday morning with his coworkers, shouting: "Thank God it's Friday!" and thinking to himself that if it wasn't for his mother, there wouldn't *be* a Friday. In fact, *Friday* comes from the old English and means "the day of Frigg," which is another name for Venus. Besides being the son of the inventor of Friday, Cupid is also the son of an Italian mom, as Venus (*Venere* in Italian) is a Roman goddess. Being the son of an Italian mom brings many other considerations, because Italian mothers are well known for their close relationships with their sons.

While Cupid's coworkers are welcoming the weekend with a loud cheer, Cupid might as well say, "Happy Mother's Day." It's great to see how much admiration your mother gets, but it can also be frustrating at times. Italian mothers can be overwhelming because they're so protective and involved. A conversation between Cupid and Venus might go like this:

"Cupid, did you eat lunch today?"

"Of course, Mom."

"What did you eat?"

"Mom, I had a sandwich. I was in a hurry to get back to work."

"Cupid, how is this possible? A sandwich? No wonder you're losing weight. Tonight I'm going to make you a nice dinner, and you can take the leftovers to work tomorrow."

"Mom, I am *not* taking it to work if it's polenta with baccala (codfish). Last time I brought that to work, the entire office had to be evacuated due to the smell. And I'm in perfect shape, by the way."

"No, you're not. Didn't I hear you coughing earlier? I should check if you have a fever."

"I don't have a fever. Why would I?"

"I keep telling you not to go outside the house with your wet hair! No wonder you get sick. I just washed your scarf, and I put it in your closet. Put it around your neck before you leave the house. This cold winter wind could give you pneumonia."

An Italian mom is the ultimate parent: she makes the best food, does your laundry, provides endless affection (although it's not confined to the house, but rather publicly displayed as well). However, problems may arise when you decide to go to college or move to the opposite side of the country. An Italian mother will do everything in her power to persuade you that you have closer options. She's just not ready to give you up. Will she ever?

Another issue is your girlfriend. An Italian mother will scrutinize her from head to toe followed by an interrogation addressing every action she's taken since birth. Typical questions would be: *Can you cook? How well? Where? Who taught you?* This is just a sample of many questions with the same objective: to determine if she's fit to become the wife of her beloved son. It's not that she's expecting your girlfriend to cook any better than she does, because that is practically impossible. She just wants to make sure that the girlfriend can make a decent version of Bolognese sauce, lasagna, eggplant parmigiana, and his favorite dish of all, pasta e fagioli. An Italian mother will never stop cooking for her son, even after he gets married. She will either literally move in with the new couple or send them a variety of sauce jars to last them a while.

And here we have Cupid, who has the best food among all the gods, and is well taken care of by his mom, Venus, who happens to be a superstar. In fact, Venus is the most beautiful among the goddesses and is worshipped by the Romans as their inspiring muse and protector of beauty and love. On the other hand, Cupid doesn't have a father. In many frescoes and paintings, Cupid is depicted next to Mars, but it's unknown if Mars is his real father. This makes complete sense. The Romans had a saying: *Mater semper certa est*, meaning that we always know who the mother is, but not necessarily who the father is. There weren't paternity tests in ancient Rome.

Cupid is depicted with a bow and arrow, which represents his source of power. Those who are shot by Cupid's arrow fall in love with the first person they see, filling them with uncontrollable desire. I always thought that Cupid had one of the coolest jobs. In Italian we say that "God makes them— referring to people—and then puts them together." Cupid's job is to fulfill the destiny of every man and woman to fall in love and procreate, ensuring the continuation of humankind. Love is what makes the world go 'round. Cupid's job is not only fun but carries some hefty responsibility. No wonder he's a workaholic. He must spread so much love around that he never takes time to get some for himself. One day, things were going to change. . . .

> Psyche was an ancient princess. She was so beautiful that men were intimidated by her radiance and began worshipping her as a deity. Psyche was a simple girl who wanted to be normal like her sisters, but beauty became an obstacle in her daily life. Meanwhile,

unbeknownst to Psyche, she was taking attention away from Venus, who became rather jealous. Venus was a caring mother but also a powerful goddess. Having titles such as the Queen of Love and Desire can get to your head. Imagine being the top model and spokeswoman for Victoria's Secret, and then, out of nowhere, Gisele Bündchen shows up. Now, you have competition and must work twice as hard to get the attention of the media.

Venus was spending countless hours in front of the mirror, double-checking her curves and makeup. In lieu of Botox, she had her lips stung by a million bees. Bad hair days were not an option. She struggled to sleep due to her constant stress. But what if she could get rid of Psyche, Tonya Harding–style, and go back to being the only attraction in town?

Venus asked Cupid to make Psyche fall in love with a terrible man, who would take her far away from the public scene. Cupid was a nice, clueless guy who reluctantly obeyed his mother. But when he saw Psyche, he was surprised by her pure beauty, stung his finger with his arrow, and fell in love. This didn't make Venus happy, but after countless therapy sessions and an intervention from the Council of the Gods, Cupid and Psyche were finally allowed to get married. The wedding ceremony—depicted by famed Renaissance painter Rafael—brought closure to the misadventures of the couple, who lived happily ever after.

Fairy tales end just like that, leaving you to wonder what really happened after the wedding. But we do know about

Cupid and Psyche. He went back to work, and Psyche had to deal with her Italian mother-in-law. She was smart enough to slightly overcook the pasta and burn the roast beef so that Venus would feel superior, thus helping their relationship. Believe me, when you know where you stand in an Italian family, it's better to just keep the peace. Cupid and Psyche had a daughter, Voluptas, who's also known as Delight, or the Goddess of Pleasures.

For centuries, Cupid continued to match countless couples, keeping the world rolling in and out of bed. Today, Cupid has offices all over the world, and has been successful in securing a love holiday on the calendar, which is celebrated on February 14. He calls it Saint Valentine's Day, a day celebrated by many to admire the famous angel who rocked a bow and arrow.

For me, the sparkle that initiated my relationships truly came from the intervention of Cupid. One day I was talking to a friend of mine, Fabrizio, whom I hadn't seen for a while. The conversation slowly but surely ended up on the topic of love. I spoke with him about my frustration in dating, and how challenging it was to find a good match. I had also joined several clubs, including spiritual churches, but Cupid didn't seem to cooperate with me.

Then, Fabrizio interrupted me, saying, "Sam, where have you been all this time? People don't meet anymore in bars. Have you heard of online dating?"

I'd heard of it but had refused to even attempt it. My reasoning was based on a simple observation: How could Cupid, the God of Love, with his bow and arrow in tow, make me fall in love with a photo on a computer screen? It didn't make sense. Love was partly a physical connection, and there was no way that an arrow of love could travel through cyberspace. Cupid was as old as the Romans and had been around since Italians lived in trees. How could he possibly adapt to this new technology?

I said to Fabrizio, "Seriously, online dating? How will it work if I don't get to really talk to the girl? How do I express love through a text or email?"

Fabrizio shook his head, "Believe me, Cupid has stepped up to the plate. He took all the online classes required to make it happen. He even has an app that you can download on your phone. Try it. Go home, create a profile, upload a few pictures, and see what happens."

I responded, "Fabrizio, I'm not sure I can. It feels so weird. It's like ordering lasagna with béchamel and meat ragu on www.lasagna.com. I like to eat my lasagna at a restaurant, talk to the waiter, possibly go into the kitchen and meet with the chef."

Fabrizio continued smiling and said, "Sam, give it a try. Just see what happens. If it doesn't work out, go back to your old system, the hit-me-with-the-arrow-Cupido system. Okay? Promise me you'll try."

That night I went home and reluctantly started up the computer, created a basic profile, and embarked on my first online dating experience. The very next day I got a message. I couldn't figure out if it was from a real person and if she was in San Diego or New Zealand. Never mind, she was probably from Alaska.

Was I going to order myself a customized girlfriend?

Is this The Girlfriend Inc?
Where I can place an order
For the best girlfriend ever,
With all the qualities I imagined
In my dreams for countless years?
I'd like her to be smart and pretty,
Outgoing, spirited, and funny,
And let me think some more,
Although I don't pretend
She is perfect without flaws,
As I have some myself.

Cupid

You're right, you've got some flaws,
And that is why I am going to call
The Hedge Fund Boyfriend Inc.,
Where they try to make the impossible possible,
To find a man for a woman
That is a faithful friend
That treats her right,
And knows that she is always right,
Makes her laugh and has class,
Tells her that she steals the act,
That she'll always be his pussycat.

Love . . . love . . . love . . .where are you, Cupid, when I need you the most?

Back Home with
Mom and Dad

⁓

After living in the United States for some time, I went back to visit my family in Italy for a few weeks. Parting from my roots had made me a different man. However, this transformation seemed to dissipate quickly once I visited my folks. A few hours after my arrival, I was thrown back in time, as if I'd never left. My parents still lived in the house where I'd spent my teenage years. Little had changed since I'd said goodbye to them. The furniture, paintings, and even the plants outside the balcony hadn't moved. I felt like a little boy again. Even the food was the same. My mom was still cooking her famously delicious dishes.

A few days before my arrival, my mom asked me what I was craving the most. And sure enough, the dinner following my arrival included all the dishes I'd asked for. To determine my cravings wasn't an easy task, as I had to choose from many of my favorites. Eventually I would have to make up my mind and opt for the classic Tuscan crostini, pappardelle with meat sauce, baked potatoes, and salad. The dessert was always a surprise.

When I arrived at the airport, I was greeted by a crowd of relatives. I can't count the number of kisses I received in just a few minutes with my family. "Come here. Let me see. You lost weight. What do you eat in America? Ahhh, Madonna Santa. Holy Mary. Hamburgers and fried potatoes aren't good for you. Let's go. You have some good food waiting for you, okay? You have to make up for all this time." Then, more kisses and hugs.

The drive from the airport to my parents' house was only thirty minutes. As soon I walked through the hall, I could smell the aromas coming from the kitchen. Usually I would have time to settle in my bedroom, look at the books in the library, and have flashbacks of when I used to read in bed and fall asleep thinking of the next day's lesson at school or the excitement of where I would be clubbing with my friends.

Finally, my mom called everybody to the table. "It's ready. Let's eat." In a few minutes, my stomach was going to get shocked by the amount of food I would have during the long dinner. My poor stomach—it would grow two sizes!

The dinner started with the antipasto. Tuscan crostini are made of hardened bread; lightly soaked in stock; and topped with a spread made from chicken liver, cream, and spices. Crostini are accompanied by sliced prosciutto or finocchiona, a typical Tuscan salami prepared with pork meat and aromatized with fennel seeds and red wine. The pasta dish was pappardelle, which are flat, wide noodles paired with my mom's homemade meat sauce. Then the main course—yes, we made it to the main course: saltimbocca alla romana, thin-cut veal chops wrapped with sage and a slice of prosciutto, sautéed spinach, and red radicchio salad. But it wasn't over. Out came the dessert, one of my favorites: biscotti di Prato, almond cookies immersed in Vin Santo, a sweet wine made from raisins. To conclude, a shot of grappa, recommended to help the digestion and assure a good night's sleep.

In the days following my arrival, the amount and variety of food on the table didn't diminish. Another favorite of mine is cacciucco, or fish soup, whose preparation requires the culinary patience of both my dad and my mother, because she was the one who had to clean up after my dad had trashed the kitchen. But all is forgiven with a plate of cacciucco, my father's signature dish for special occasions.

Cacciucco originated in Livorno, a province of Tuscany and the main port of the region. There's a legend about this dish:

> A fisherman went out to sea one day but was met with a violent tempest and died. He left his wife and children in misery. They had no choice but to ask for food. The children went to all the fishermen in the port of Livorno, who were moved by the tragedy of the poor family, and gave to each of the children a fish: calamari, octopus, mussels, clams, scorpionfish, shrimps, gurnards, red mullets, and many other Mediterranean creatures. When they got back home, the mother prepared a soup with every fish, adding onions, tomatoes, leeks, and other vegetables she had in the house; and for the final touch, garlic, red pepper, thyme, a bay leaf, and parsley. She poured the soup in a bowl next to a plate of sliced garlic bread. The soup was enough to satisfy the family and to feed the fishermen as well, as the aroma of the soup had traveled to the foodies, or *buongustai*, of the village.

Just like the lady who first cooked cacciucco ended up feeding the entire village, my dad could do the same, as he has never been great when it comes to measuring quantities. His philosophy is "the more the better." He would make cacciucco in quantities far exceeding our large appetites. So, at the end of the dinner, there were always leftovers for the rest of the week. Luckily, my dad had a good job that provided for my family, and cacciucco was only made for very special occasions. Otherwise, he may as well have filed for bankruptcy after cooking the dish, and his children would have had to go to the fishermen to beg for some charity.

Another great dish prepared by my dad is panzanella, a culinary delight served during the summer. It doesn't require lots of preparation and is quite inexpensive—great to make after the lavish cacciucco. Panzanella is a cold dish made with Tuscan bread and vegetables. The origin of this staple of Tuscan cuisine dates to the beginning of Italy, as it's mentioned in the poetry of several Florentine writers of the Renaissance. It came from the practice of farmers wetting stale bread to make it soft and adding vegetables from their gardens. Panzanella is served in place of pasta or as an appetizer. My dad uses fresh vegetables including tomatoes, onions, cucumbers, red radicchio, celery, and capers; and then he adds tuna and hard-boiled eggs, topping it off with olive oil, salt, and pepper.

Living in California allowed me to meet a variety of people from different cultures and countries. I didn't have to make a strenuous effort to look for some foreign cuisine. In Italy, it was difficult to find a sushi restaurant or a taco shop—— although things have been rapidly changing in recent years. In California, not only can one can find any kind of food, but also any kind of religion, clothing style, and anything else you may think of. Weird is cool in California. In fact, the weirder, the better. This shouldn't surprise anyone, as Hollywood is right around the corner.

When I started my first job in San Diego, I became close friends with Luis, a slightly older, classy Mexican man. His kindness earned him the respect of everybody in the company. In addition, he had great style and was very composed, no matter what the situation. I liked going into his office to chat and get advice. One day we went out to lunch together, and I was surprised to find out that he was vegetarian. Not only did he choose this lifestyle for health reasons, but mostly because he was Hindu. Now, how could I tell my family that I was friends with a vegetarian Mexican Hindu who was the manager at the golf company I worked for? It wouldn't make sense to my dad, who lived in the stereotypical Italian society of that time. He had never met a Hindu, and had definitely never met a vegetarian. A Mexican vegetarian Hindu golfer. Never mind. Is he gay? No. That would have been even more odd, as it was another variant that wasn't familiar to my folks.

Eventually, Luis invited me to go to a Hindu temple with his family, which I gladly did. It was my first experience with another religion other than Catholicism. Over the next few months, I started meditating and then became a vegetarian. I went so far as to become a vegan for nearly a year. I was eating tofurky, veggie sausages, and vegetarian bologna. I also joined a raw-food group and met the most unusual people, friends that I would have never imagined making in my life. I met a guy known as the "hug man," who envisioned starting a business that would involve giving hugs in exchange for money. Or how about the guy who wanted to rent a room in my house in exchange for making me a green smoothie every day? Or the psychologist for animals, a guy who seemed to be gifted in talking to depressed cats, dogs, parrots—you name it.

My life had dramatically changed, but being vegetarian in California was effortless. Almost every restaurant in San Diego, even a steakhouse, had a vegetarian option. If I invited any of my new friends to a party at my house, nobody was surprised by my being different. But honestly, what is different? What are the parameters that establish what is different? Well, it all depends from which perspective you're speaking. If I'd introduced my dad to the animal psychologist, he would say: "That's different! Can he talk to crickets too? Because there's one in the house that doesn't want to leave and keeps me up at night." But I was getting used to a place where infinite possibilities were a daily reality.

Summer came. I was going to visit my family again. I was so excited . . . but wait . . . how could I possibly tell my family that I wasn't going to eat osso buco, prosciutto, and cacciucco?

I knew that they wouldn't be pleased with such an announcement. I was dreading that call from my mom asking me what I'd been craving since my last visit. She was ready to cook for me as soon as I walked through the door.

"Mom, can you make me some kale salad, lentil soup, and soy sausage with rice cauliflower? For dessert, I can have anything as long as it's dairy-, egg-, gelatin-, and cruelty-free. No GMOs, and don't cook in the same oven where you cook the meat." If I'd told my mom anything of the sort, she would collapse to the floor; and as soon as she'd recovered from fainting, she'd call the Italian Embassy and instruct them to put me on the first flight back home. Perhaps she would have come herself to pick me up, grab me by one ear, and take me back home: "You are *not* going back to that *grullaio* [madhouse] called America!"

Becoming vegetarian was one of the most challenging things to deal with now that I was going back home. I thought of several different scenarios to predict my family's reaction. I considered not going back at all. How long was I going to keep this secret? I could tell them the doctor had ordered me to go on a vegetarian diet due to a one-in-a-million disease that I'd contracted from a McDonald's hamburger— but how could I have possibly eaten at McDonald's? That was already a sacrilege for anybody in my family! I would have to go to the priest, confess, and ask for God's forgiveness. Or I could argue that Jesus didn't eat meat, and I was on a journey to imitate Christ and become a more spiritual person. Are we kidding? Jesus was a foodie; not only did he multiply fish, but he made sure there was enough wine at the Wedding at Cana. Certainly no other excuse would work. Ultimately, even if I'd found a good one, my mom would say that the Italian food cooked by her would heal any of my ailments. Indeed, she would insist that this problem had arisen because I'd left home and had ventured into the strange culinary territory of America.

Then, I had an idea. Maybe I could share some books with my family, such us *Small Planet* or *Fast Food Nation*; or tell them about some famous historical vegetarians such as Gandhi, Virgil, and Tolstoy. I could add that I was trying to reduce the worldwide population of cows, whose farting contributed to global warming and the hole in the ozone layer. But I knew that not even this excuse would work. Especially the cows farting too much. My family would say that grandpa's farts had already determined the fate of the ozone a long time ago.

I decided to write a long email explaining that I'd become a vegetarian because I was old enough to decide what I wanted to eat, and thanks in advance for your support, but I'm not going to eat any animal products when I sit down at the table, so don't insist or make me feel guilty. . . blah, blah, blah. . . .

My father replied to my email with a simple "Okay." This was interesting. I hadn't expected that. I was ready for fighting and my mother crying uncontrollably. Hmm . . .

There was no additional discussion about the topic between the delivery of my email and my arrival in Italy. I booked my first flight with a special request for a vegetarian meal. I'd never done that before. I couldn't believe how prepared the airlines were for any special meal request. I could have even requested a Hindu or Kosher meal or Paleo meat. I wish they'd offered vegan Italian: lasagna made with zucchini and tofu ricotta, but they hadn't gone that far yet.

I was glad I was flying Lufthansa because I didn't have the courage to see how the Italian airline was coping with these requests, or if they even bothered trying. The food on any airplane isn't that great, but because flying overseas makes you bored and on edge, even the boxed meals can become an exciting break from the torture of being stuck in your seat. One time, the passenger sitting in front of me was an older Asian gentleman who didn't speak English, and it took what seemed like half an hour for the flight attendant to make him understand that the choices were either pasta or chicken. She also had to simulate a chicken with her arms to make her point. I admired and empathized with the flight attendants who had so much patience.

After thirteen hours in the air, I arrived at the Florence airport. My parents and the same crowd of assorted relatives came to greet me and take me home. The thirty minutes from the airport to my parents' home was not the same as before. I was tense. Not my parents—they were just fine. I was thinking about when dinner would be served. I knew something was up. I had to defend the honor of my new vegetarian "religion." I wouldn't let anybody attack my garden of fresh vegetables. Not even my family. Maybe they had prepared even more amazing food to tempt me. The lasagna would have looked like a demon to me, a Satan to be addressed with exorcism: "Leave me alone, lasagna Bolognese, my soul is strong, and I will resist you. I will not sin. I will pray to the goddesses Kale and Zucchini, who will free me from your ungodly meat."

I saw myself sitting at the table talking in a Shakespearean tone, telling those around me: "Look at this lamb cooked in white wine, and look at this asparagus covered in parmesan. Look at this steak cooked with my mom's sauce; and look at this carrot, boiled and dressed with salt and pepper. To be or not to be? To eat or not to eat? To sin or not to sin. To forget or not to forget a life filled with veggie meals?" I was so glad that Hamlet didn't have to deal with as much pain as I did, sitting in front of the pasta puttanesca with anchovies, the abbachio, and the Marengo cake.

Then, the moment of truth came. Angels and demons were laid out on the table. My dad said the prayer, "Thank you, God, for gathering us all together around this table, for the good food and the good appetite that you provided us. In the name of the Father, the Son, and the Holy Spirit. Enjoy your meal."

The invocation was followed by my mom saying, "*Mangia,* please, help yourself." Then she turned to me and asked, "What are you going to eat?"

"I will have some of the grilled polenta with sautéed mushrooms."

"What about some prosciutto? This is from the farmer's market. It was just picked up this morning."

"No, Mom. I will pass on that."

"Do as you want; the food is here."

The dinner went on just like that, with the offering of food and my opting for the vegetarian selections that were available. My mom, somehow, had made an effort to have something for me, in case she couldn't convince me.

The dinner was finally over. I'd managed to make it through unscathed. I got up from the table and went in the living room to relax on the sofa. My mom brought me a chamomile tea to ease the jet lag and ensure a good night's sleep.

"Did you become a Buddhist?" she asked.

"What do you mean?" I replied.

"Why don't you eat meat? You must have lost your mind in America and joined some Buddhist group."

"Mom, what does Buddhism have to do with not eating meat?"

"Well, what's his name, that big celebrity on television? Isn't he Buddhist and preaching left and right not to eat animals?"

"Mom, what are you talking about?"

"Son, you're forgetting about Jesus."

"No, I'm not. Jesus is still in my life."

"So, then, why aren't you going to church anymore? I think that you've been brainwashed in America. All these crazy people . . . and the more time you spend there, the crazier you'll get."

"America, church, Buddha . . . Mom, how many topics are we talking about? What do they have to do with each other?"

"They all have a common denominator: you. You've changed."

"Mom, of course I've changed. I'm growing up. I hope I'm changing for the better and taking care of myself. Besides, I'm becoming who I aspire to be."

"Without eating meat? Is that how you're becoming who you want to be? I'm telling you, one of these days, this vegetarian idea of yours will make you sick."

"Sick?"

"Yes, sick. Soy sauce and spring rolls don't make good blood. It's like trying to make wine out of water."

"Jesus did that."

"My son, you need food of substance to stay healthy and strong. Look at those skinny Buddhist monks! Not to mention those skinny cows wandering around the streets of India. I can't believe they let that meat wander around while they die of starvation."

"Mom, that's their religion. The cow is sacred to them."

"Let me make them some sacred lasagna or pappardelle Bolognese and they'll quickly change their minds."

"Okay, now you're telling me that you can change the traditions of an entire nation with a cook-off?"

"Whatever it takes to make this world have some common sense."

"Are we talking about the common sense of your cooking?"

"Why not? Didn't Italians make the world a better place by spreading the concept of *la dolce vita*?"

"I'm not sure everyone would agree with you. The sweet life is made with the acceptance that the world is varied and beautiful just the way it is. It's a mixed green salad with a little bit of everything."

"I think eating vegetables are making you think too much. *Diavolino* . . . the little devil is working hard to confuse you."

"Oh my gosh, Mom, you're one of a kind."

"Yes, and you better eat some meat. I'm going to make your favorite tomorrow: pappardelle al sugo di chinghiale — wild boar meat sauce. Chinghiale, not chipotle . . ."

I'm surprised I survived that summer vacation, but I stood by my new lifestyle and successfully remained a vegetarian after two weeks of food bombardment from left and right.

I returned to America and continued to eat my tofurky and fake bologna. I was an active participant in a vegan blog and kept hanging out with my friends "hug man" and "animal-psychologist guy." One day a big fight exploded on the vegan blog. Insults started flying from one member to the other. It continued for days. The fight was about garlic. Was garlic healthy or not? If you ate garlic, you were stupid. You didn't eat garlic? Then you didn't know what you were missing. It was in the midst of this garlic war that I decided that vegetarianism was no longer for me. I really believed that being vegetarian was my true contribution to a better world, but I realized that any label that makes you think you're better than somebody else is the antithesis of progress. And since I didn't want to be labeled or label others based on their garlic preferences, I decided on the spot to quit and go back to eating meat.

My mom was so relieved when she heard the news.

"I'm back to eating lasagna Bolognese and bistecca alla fiorentina—steak Florentine-style."

The next time I went back home to visit my family, my mom served me my favorite dish and said, "I'm so happy. Let's forget about all this Buddha stuff and have some nice meat loaf!"

The Pope

*It's 6 a.m. I'm staring at Michelangelo's sculpture of the Madonna with Christ, knowns as *Pietà*, in a completely empty church. Then, a friend of mine calls me and says, "Let's go." A few seconds later, I'm running in the central nave of the Cathedral of Saint Peter, in Vatican City. I can hear the echo of my shoes clapping on the marble floor and reverberating in the massive emptiness of a living museum of Renaissance and Baroque art. I am eleven years old. It wasn't a dream. I was there.

It all began two years before.

It was one of those summer nights when the crickets were singing their lullabies and jumping from one pine tree to the other. It was hot. The evening brought in a breeze from the window to relieve my sweaty skin. It was around 8 p.m., and I was sitting with my family on the sofa in the living room. The mahogany table at our home was covered with an elegant cloth and set for dinner. We were waiting for a close friend of our family, Father Damiano, a priest of the order of Saint Dominic.

My father had gone to pick him up at the church of Pistoia, a town twenty minutes away from my house, where Father Damiano had retired. They arrived a few minutes later. Father Damiano was dressed in his white cream robe and black belt, sandals, and a hat, that, once removed, revealed his bald head. He wore a pair of glasses that framed two playful eyes, similar to those of a child preparing to do something silly and then running away afterward.

Father Damiano was a funny person in addition to being a well-respected theology scholar; he'd taught for many years at a university in Rome. I'll never forget when, one day, he brought me a vinyl record with several children's songs; we played all of them and sang along. My favorite was the Pinocchio song: "Dear Pinocchio, friend of my happiest days, with all of the secrets that I trusted in you . . . Dear Pinocchio, do you remember when I was a child? In my white pajamas, as I looked at you, flipping through your book and dreamed with you . . ." It was on that night that Father Damiano was going to change the course of my life. I was nine years old.

My mom and my grandma were bringing to the table the many courses for the night when at some point everybody got quiet. I don't remember what we ate, but if we were quiet, even for a short period of time, the food must have been very good. Talking could wait. Then, Father Damiano interrupted the silence:

"Samuele, how is it going at school?"

"I like it. We're studying Giacomo Leopardi right now."

"He's a great poet. Melancholic, but he remains one of the best poets of our time."

"I had to learn 'Saturday in the Village' by memory."

"I also had to learn that poem by memory. Can you recite it for us?"

I went on to say the poem in front of my family.

"The damsel from the field returns,
The sun is sinking in the west;
Her bundle on her head she sets,
And in her hand she bears
A bunch of roses and violets.
Tomorrow is a holiday . . ."

"Do you know what the poem is about?" Father Damiano asked me.

"Yes, Leopardi compares youth to Saturday, the day to feast."

"You're living the full bloom of your youth; do you know that? Don't get old. It comes with wisdom but also with many other undesirable symptoms."

What was he talking about? What could youth and wisdom possibly mean to a nine-year-old?

Father Damiano continued. "I remember when I was nine like you and going out with my friends to the fields around my parents' house in Nocera Umbra. We harvested hazelnuts from the trees, broke the shells, and ate the nuts. Then, we ran after each other with a stick and pretended we were the three musketeers."

I said, "We have many pines here. I went with Grandma to get the pine nuts, and we made a big stack. Then we made pesto with them. That is the pesto we had tonight."

"That was excellent. No wonder it was so good. It had that taste of . . . I know . . . that your grandma loves you very much." And he smiled at me and my grandmother. He was right. She did love me. We would spend entire afternoons together under those tall trees, gathering pines, looking for the fruit inside, and hammering on them to get the precious nuts out of the shell, the indispensable ingredient in pesto.

He continued. "I want to tell you about a school that I know to be very special."

"A school?"

"A middle school for when you finish fifth grade."

"Is it here in Prato?"

"No, it's not here. It's in Vatican City, and it's the Pope's favorite school."

"The Polish Pope? He's cool. Do you know that he was shot by a terrorist not too long ago?"

"Yes, I know. That's because he's a good man, and he's trying hard to free millions of people from the struggle of the communist ideology, an ideology that has failed."

"My dad told me that communists are morons."

Father Damiano laughed. Again, what could I possibly know about communists and ideologies?

"The school I'm talking about is a boarding school. You have to live there. You'll be back during Christmas and Easter holidays and during the summer. You can go there once you turn eleven."

"In two years?"

"Yes, when you start sixth grade. The school has thirty students, about ten for each class. Therefore, every year they accept ten new students. I could put in a good word for you if you're interested."

"But do I have to live there? Can I come back home after school?"

"Rome is three hours away from Florence, and therefore, you'll have to live at the school. Then, every morning, you'll serve the Mass inside the Cathedral of Saint Peter. You're going to be one of the Pope's altar boys. Seven days a week. The church is open every day, and the Pope doesn't take time off. He's a busy guy, and you're going to help him. You'll also take turns with the other students to serve him Mass on Sundays."

"I'm going to be friends with the Pope?"

"Yup! Not bad. What do you think?"

"That is so cool."

"Think about this opportunity, and once you finish fifth grade, we can talk about it some more. But you must keep up with your grades and continue to study Leopardi. Next time you can recite me another poem. Okay?"

"Sure, I'll recite you 'S'I' fosse foco' (If I were fire) by Cecco Angiolieri."

That night, a seed was sown in my head: a boarding school with children dressed in uniform, who were friends of the Pope. Neither my father nor my mother paid too much attention to that conversation, and I figured I would forget all about it in two years. Besides, how could I live far away from home? That's not the fate of an Italian child—especially, a boy. An Italian boy lives with his mom until he gets married. That's why he's a mommy's boy. An Italian mother has to feed her son with all the good stuff until he's ready to get married to his wife, who's been well trained to cook for him. By who? By the mother-in-law, of course! No way was that conversation with Father Damiano going anywhere. Was he trying to convince me to become a priest? Even then, I wasn't going to leave my home before I was an adult and had enough of my mom's affection. . . . And was I going to leave the house even then?

Nobody in the rest of the family paid any attention to the exchange between Father Damiano and me that night, either. Therefore, it came as a surprise when, two year later, the topic of the Pope's school in Vatican City was exhumed from the darkness. One night when Father Damiano came to dinner at our home, I asked him if I could go and see the school. My parents must have talked in private with Father Damiano, and he must have reassured them about the school's good reputation. He must have tried especially hard with my mother, who was difficult to convince, because any school that would be the cause of her son being taken away from her couldn't possibly be any good. She may have even thought about moving with me, but that wasn't an option.

In July of 1982, I turned eleven. September came upon us fast, and it was time for me to join the Pope's school and become an Angel of Saint Peter's Cathedral. The Sunday morning of my departure for Rome is still vivid in my mind. I woke up with the glare of the sun filtering through the curtains in my bedroom. I looked at the boundless plowed field in front of my house as a flock of doves flew by. I identified with them, as they were so used to traveling long distances. I was also going to travel to a new destination and leave the house where I grew up for the first time. My feelings were mixed—I felt both excitement and fear.

I went to the kitchen still wearing my pajamas. My mom was busy preparing breakfast. She didn't show any signs of sadness, but I could see her mouth trembling slightly. I saw my luggage sitting beside the door, and I knew that inside those suitcases lay the sadness of my mother, who'd placed my clothes layer after layer, almost as if she hoped that the luggage wouldn't fill up and she wouldn't have to close them and let me go. The quiet of that morning was that of an approaching tornado, of a closed dam that doesn't allow the natural spring water to flow into the ocean. The school in Vatican wasn't on the other side of the world, but for my mother to see her eleven-year-old son leaving home was very hard. I was the last son, the little one, the one who, probably, she'd held on to more than the others, hesitating to cut the umbilical cord.

I'd made a decision that was at odds with the rest of my peers. I was leaving the stability and affection of my home to embark on an adventure whose successful outcome wasn't guaranteed. Looking back at those days, I'm sure that my mother and my father had long and animated discussions behind their bedroom doors. Why was my father going along with my request? How could an eleven-year-old make a decision of such importance? Move two hundred and fifty miles away, live with complete strangers, and be separated from the rest of the family? How about the nun's school just a few blocks down the street? Why couldn't I go to that middle school, instead?

Before I jumped in the car, I looked at the fields in front of my home. In my mind, I greeted the farmer who would be harvesting the grapes, the cats that swarmed in front of the barnyard, and the chicks following their mothers under the watchful eyes of the cock. I was happy and excited to start a new chapter in my life, to make new friends, to meet the Polish Pope, and to go to *Roma Capoccia*—Rome the Big Head—the capital of Italy and the ancient world.

The car was speeding down highway A11, which connects Florence to Rome. The freeway carves through the Apennines, the mountain range that extends along the length of the peninsula. Entering the tunnels along the freeway gave me a thrill. The orange lights inside the tunnels were breaking and flashing on the windshield, and it felt like being inside the sleeping body of a giant creature.

We arrived in Rome after three hours. We took the Lungotevere, and then Via della Conciliazione. Suddenly, the Cathedral of Saint Peter stood in front of me with its splendor and majesty. We turned left after the colonnade, and then we stopped at the gate to enter Vatican City. Two Swiss guards with their multicolored uniforms were on opposite sides of the gate, while the third approached us and asked my father where we were headed. Upon saying, "Preseminario San Pio X," the Swiss guard let us in.

The back of the cathedral, which I was seeing for the first time, looked like the posterior of a woman with her head resting on her lifted leg. At that moment, I imagined the great artists of the Renaissance walking on this same street, going to see the Pope to bring him the plans for their latest updated building projects. A few blocks away, we encountered another checkpoint where Vatican guards stood. They also requested the purpose of our visit and directed us to follow the street straight ahead and then pass underneath the arch connecting the cathedral to the palace of the rectory. We cut through Saint Martha's Square and took the street parallel to the train station, next to the Governorate, the warehouse of Vatican City. Then we parked the car in the back of Palazzo Saint Carlo, my new home.

My father and my brother Leonardo, who'd come along, helped me carry my suitcases inside the dormitory. My bed was the last on the corner of the biggest dorm on the second floor. My parents spoke with one of the priests at the school, and then we all walked outside to say goodbye. Of course, my mother started crying, almost as if she were possessed. She couldn't stop holding onto me. It took all the strength of my father to make her walk to the parking lot. With one last goodbye wave, they all got inside the car and left, and I started to walk back inside.

As I entered the little door in the back, I turned for a second and looked back at the street until my father's car wasn't visible anymore. From inside the boarding school, I could hear some piano music. I wondered if that music was going to be the soundtrack of my experience as the Pope's altar boy. As I would learn soon, my life at the school would not only be marked by music that was in tune, but also by discordant notes—those of my maturation, of bullying peers, and of priests preaching . . . but not practicing what they preached.

Something was fishy at the Vatican. Living at the epicenter of Christianity made me see how incongruent the church's teachings were in contrast to the reality of its actions. I was annoyed by the flood of money that I saw passing hands in the sacristy of Saint Peter. Many Popes in history had been controversial and thirsty for power. I didn't have to go as far back as Alexander VI Borgia. During my stay, the news covered the scandal of the Banco Ambrosiano, the biggest Italian financial institution that along with the assent of the Vatican, was involved in money laundering with the Mob. But John Pope II was a good guy; I'm sure about that. He didn't have anything to do with all this madness. I was a true believer that he got involved in that mess without having any clue about what was actually going on.

During my three years in Vatican City, I met John Paul II several times. On one occasion, the students along with their parents were invited to a papal audience, where I expressed my gratitude to the Pope for encouraging youth to be more involved in the church—the good church—not the one that was making deals with the Mafia. When I left for the United States, John Paul was still there, older, but still in charge of the shack. I imagined having a conversation with him. . . .

> "Hey, Pope John, can I call you that? Or do you prefer Karl? After all, we're friends. I'm

getting a little bit edgy here in Italy. I love my home country, but things don't seem to get any better. I have a sense that what is happening at the Vatican and in Rome is the same thing that happened to the Roman senate two thousand years ago: corruption led to new corruption, and the empire eventually collapsed. People don't realize that the world is rapidly changing, and Italy is sitting back waiting for another train to stop by. Albert Einstein's famous quote about 'doing the same thing over and over again but expecting different results' seems to be most appropriate for the present condition in which we're living. Don't get me wrong, I'm going to miss my family, the food, the wine, and so much artistic and natural beauty, but I don't see any other choice than to experience the freedom of America. What do you think?"

"South America?"

"No, the United States."

"What are you going to do in a Protestant country? Martin Luther and the Reformation gave us quite a few problems."

"Of course, Martin Luther wanted to read the Bible and interpret it on its own. Why should the Pope always have the last word? I'm out of here. . . see you in California?"

"I can't. I'm stuck here."

"Okay. Give me a call anytime. And good luck with resolving those scandals . . . I know you didn't have anything to do with that. Oh, and I wanted to ask you, isn't it time you trade in that boring old Popemobile for a blazing-red Fiat? I have just the one for you!"

"No way, I only drive Mercedes. But wait. That would be perfect for my uncle Igor."

"You got it. Sold! Just tell Igor to bring the car to Tony's for a tune-up and fix it again, because there's always something to be fixed with a Fiat."

Eventually, I had a moment of clarity. To make the shift in my life, I had to leave my family one more time, just like I had when I was eleven years old. But this time I was twenty-six. I said goodbye to the Pope, my family, and my country.

America, here I come. . . .

Alexa

One Sunday morning I was lying in bed checking my phone. I saw that I didn't have any emails, texts, or missed calls. Then I called out to my Amazon virtual assistant, Alexa.

"Alexa, good morning, how are you doing? Can you play some pop music?"

Alexa was quiet.

"Alexa, are you okay? Did I wake you up too early?"

I thought that maybe she wanted me to give her more specific instructions, so I tried: "Alexa, can you play a Mozart concerto in G major?" Silence. Perhaps she was mad at me. Had I wished her a good night before I'd fallen asleep? She might've thought I was a jerk for telling her to shut up when she started laughing last night, out of nowhere. That was an overreaction on my part. After all, she's just a computer, a machine. Why should I make fun of a machine?

"Alexa, where is my underwear? Can you call my fiancée? Tell me a joke that knocks my pants off!"

She kept answering: "I'm not sure about that."

Of course you're not sure about that. You're a damn speaker connected to the internet. How could you know? Could it be that she did have a clue but was giving me the silent treatment? She was acting just like any Donatella, Francesca, Elena, Giuseppina . . . and why should I be surprised? *Alexa* ends with an *a*, like most female names in Italy. I decided that she *was* giving me the cold shoulder and that I needed to show some regret before she'd finally forgive me.

I remember when I was single, meaning "singled out" in a society that requires people to be reliable and always glued to their cell phones. If you get a text message, you have five seconds to reply. Any delay can cost you countless friendships. I'm someone who needs his space. In this sense, cell phones were a threat to me for the longest time. I refused to get a cell phone until a few years ago. The only way to get in touch with me was to call my work phone or leave a message on my home phone. Everything had to be arranged days before. I was trying to make a point: if we didn't have cell phones growing up, why were they indispensable now? But eventually I had to give up my resistance to the digital world. Upon the insistence of friends and family, I bought my first cell phone on March 16, 2014. How could I forget that day? It was when my crusade against technology ended.

I went to the closest Verizon store, and the greeter asked me what I was looking for. I told him I needed a cell phone. He asked if I needed an upgrade or if I'd lost my cell.

I told him, "I don't even know if I *want* a cell phone. I'm not here of my own volition. I was forced to come." There were a lot of people on my case. They'd told me that I was putting my life in danger without a cell phone. How could I call AAA if my car engine blew up on the freeway? (How many car engines blow up, anyway?) I told them I could do what I'd done for many years—wave at passing cars with a confident smile.

Then they asked me what would happen if I got lost at night, in the woods, in a desolate part of Montana? Again they said the cell phone would save my life. But why would I ever get lost at night in Montana? Why would I even *go* to Montana? Just to test my cell-phone emergency skills? People had lived thousands of years without cell phones, but now I wouldn't be able to survive without one? I needed to be connected with the world twenty-four hours a day?

"Sir, please take a seat, and the next available associate will be with you," said the greeter, looking at me as if I were a psychopath. I was concerned that he might call the FBI and say, "There's a suspect here without an official cell phone. I've never seen anything like this before."

After I'd wandered around the store for ten minutes, I was approached by a woman in her twenties. She had a Texan accent, long blonde hair, and she flashed a big smile. "Mr. Sam?"

"Yes, nice to meet you."

"Looks like you need a new cell phone. How can I help you?"

"I've never *had* a cell phone. I feel weird and embarrassed."

"Wow! That's interesting. Are you Amish?"

"No, but I've heard that even Amish people make exceptions and use cell phones."

"You have an accent."

"Yes, I'm Italian. I've been here many years. In Italy, we don't call each other; we meet in person. As far as making plans, people are very flexible. Time is not of the essence."

"What do you mean? A 7 p.m. appointment is a 7 p.m. appointment."

"Not in my hometown. 7 p.m. is more like 9 p.m."

"In California you can get by with some time flexibility. Not in New York. We live in a new world."

"I guess I need to get on board."

"Let's see what we have. Do you have something in mind?"

"Yes, the most basic one you have."

"You mean as far as price?"

"No, I mean as far as being on a leash 24/7."

"I know what you mean, but it's also convenient to have a way to reach out to somebody instantly."

"You mean to be at anyone's disposal anytime?"

"Here is the simplest smartphone we have."

"I was thinking about something more basic."

"Really?"

"Yes. What about that phone?" I pointed to one that didn't look complicated.

"A flip phone?"

"Flip phone. Yes, exactly that. All I need is to call people, not send video documentaries."

She looked at me, wondering if I was kidding. Flip phones are like my grandma's cuckoo clock—antiquated technology. They're only on display as a reminder of what people used in the "Neanderthal Cell Phone Era." They call them "dumb phones" or "caveman phones."

I bought one anyway and made my first "dumb" phone call. I dialed my daughter's number, which I knew by memory, something that wouldn't happen in the future, as the number would be saved in my contacts.

"Hello," she answered.

"Hi, it's me. I have a cell phone."

"Dad, you really have one?"

"Just got it now."

"What did you get? iPhone?"

"No, Blackberry."

"No way. Blackberries are obsolete. I'm surprised they even have them at the store."

"A cell phone that's already history?"

"Yes, they don't work that well."

"Sorry, it must be a boysenberry, then."

"Come on, Dad . . ."

"Just kidding. I got a Samsung."

"What kind?"

"It's a normal, easygoing phone to call people. I don't think it went to Harvard, if that's what you mean."

"Okay, I'm at school. Text me later."

"Okay. You'll have to teach me. Talk to you later."

"Ciao."

The news that I had a cell phone spread quickly. I began receiving many "Congratulations" messages. It was official: I'd joined the world of instant social gratification. However, most of the emoji and video messages I was receiving didn't come through my "dumb" phone. I resisted some more, but then, in October 2015, I gave up and got an upgrade, getting a phone that "had gone to college" and could be considered smart—not Harvard smart, more like community-college smart.

Fast-forward to today, and I have my hand wrapped around my cell phone and am talking to Alexa.

"Alexa, what's the weather like today?"

No answer.

Then it occurred to me that none of the devices were working: no cell phone, no computer, no laptop. I was disconnected from the world.

Help!

I felt like I was on a deserted island, in the middle of the ocean, miles away from civilization.

Luckily, I found the solution, or better yet, the solution found me: I'd forgotten to pay the phone and internet bill. In all this communication confusion, I hadn't set up the direct online payment. Once again, I was behind schedule when it came to technological progress. Nobody uses checks to pay bills anymore, and I had to change my ways once again. The good news is that I won't have to buy stamps for all the letters I used to send, and I can spend more time checking my phone. It used to be just a phone, but now it's my lifesaver.

Ah, what a relief! I'm back on my search engine, catching up on my texts and Facebook messages. I apologized to everybody for the late replies because I don't want to risk shrinking my Facebook followers on my journey to reach five thousand. But what's more uplifting is that Alexa is back to normal, as normal as can be. At least she's no longer mad at me!

Shoe Size

My friend PJ is Indian. He's a wine connoisseur and a chef. He dresses elegantly, is a smooth talker with women, and loves shoes. Let me repeat, he has a real passion for shoes. At his home in San Diego, he has twenty pairs of them lined up on the floor, all custom-made by artisan shoe companies in Italy. He must have Italian ancestors, or maybe he spent many previous lifetimes in Italy.

I sent a picture of my Indian/Italian friend to my dad. He asked, "Who's your Italian friend? The one standing next to you." To which I replied, "That's PJ. He acts more Italian than I do. You should consider adopting him."

In Italy, shoes are not only a necessity, but they also say a lot about your personality. When I was a teenager, I used to spend entire afternoons in downtown Florence, going from store to store to find the right shoes. They had to be comfortable, made from good material, and on trend. Shoes in Italy are as important as kale is to a vegan.

But in California, I had to deal with a new situation. Shoes were symbols of something else: trophies to be displayed for one's vanity—not because they were made by fine artisans, but because of their size, which supposedly, revealed the size of something else.

One time when I was with my girlfriend at a housewarming party in La Jolla, we took a tour of the home, which was located at the top of Mount Soledad with a stunning view of the ocean. The new owners hadn't spared a penny on their elegant furniture and decorations, including some rare paintings of one of my favorite contemporary artists. Not only did the house have a spacious kitchen and master bedroom, but also an enormous walk-in closet with two racks for shoes. I was expecting the lady of the house to have many shoes, but what a surprise to see that the husband had just as many, and maybe more. I looked at the shoes and thought to myself, *If they were my size, I would take a pair for myself. I'm sure the man of the house wouldn't mind.* But, alas, what was I going to do with a size 10? Even if they were flip-flops, my toes wouldn't fit in them.

After completing the tour, my girlfriend and I rejoined the crowd downstairs. What a fun evening! The band was playing some soft tunes; and the dining-room table was covered with plates of authentic Italian food, including an assortment of cheese and various bottles of wine, such as Antinori Chianti Riserva. The food had been prepared by a local Italian restaurant, whose owner was among the guests. It only took me a matter of seconds to find out who the Italian man was. I waited to introduce myself because he was on the phone. Meanwhile, I had the pleasure of meeting the "cheese people"—not that they were cheesy, but they were the ones who'd brought the generous plates of cheese, including some imported from Italy, France, and Spain. Nothing beats truffle cheese, pecorino, and Camembert. And if you don't dwell on the smell, gorgonzola and crackers are a great way to start a feast.

Finally, the Italian man got off the phone. I walked over to the painting he was standing in front of and said, *"Buonasera."*

"Are you Italian?" he asked me.

"No, but I like to fake being one. After all, the world is divided: the ones who are Italians and the ones who pretend to be."

"Seriously, where are you from?"

"I'm from Florence."

"No kidding. I'm from Florence as well. What a coincidence. It's not easy to meet people from Tuscany here in San Diego. Where exactly in Florence?"

"From Prato. I know . . . it's outside the walls of Florence. You know, I once met somebody in Florence who was trying to explain to me the difference between being from inside the walls and outside. It seems that the people who are born outside the walls of Florence have smelly feet. True Florentines think of us as 'inferiors.' As you know, that is part of our millennial culture of making fun of each other."

"I know. I'm Mario. I'm from inside the walls of Florence. But I have a friend in Prato. Do you know Massimo Bestione?"

"Bestione . . . doesn't ring a bell. But I hope you told him that before he comes to visit you, he better wash his feet!"

"Let's join everyone around the fireplace. I'm going to the bathroom, but I'll be right back," he told me.

"Okay, see you there."

As I waited by the fire, something unfortunate occurred. One of the guests started talking in a way that he would later regret.

"We all saw those shoes up in the closet. What size do you wear?" the unknown guest said to the party host.

"Didn't you see? I wear a ten," replied the man of the house.

"And what do you guys wear?" he asked the rest of the guys, anxious to make his point.

"I wear a ten and half," said one.

"I'm an eleven," said another.

"Oh, I think mine is the smallest—it's an eight," said the last one in the circle.

With a smirk, the guest said, "Sorry, guys, but I think I have the biggest. I'm a twelve."

It became clear that he wanted to embarrass the men in front of their female partners. Everyone started hiding their feet under their chairs to avoid further discussion.

Then, Mario came back from the bathroom and asked, "What's going on here?"

"Nothing, we were just discussing shoe sizes. I have a twelve," said the prankster, expecting to win the contest.

Mario replied, "That's great. Sometimes nature is funny. I may not be that tall, but I have a thirteen. Does that mean something?" The crowd roared with laughter. Now, the malicious guy, the one who thought he would impress the crowd with his twelve, had to hide behind a palm tree for the rest of the night.

That was quite the commotion over a number. I'm not sure who started the rumor that shoe size matters. Seriously, how can size even matter if one doesn't know how to use it? If one is skillful, the world is his. More important, he is a real man, no matter the size.

Fast Food

*I*magine finding yourself in a small village in Poland, having never spoken the language. It's lunchtime, and you're very hungry. What would you do? I found myself in a very similar situation, but I wasn't in Poland. I was in Springfield, Missouri.

It was my second day in America, and I was at my former mother-in-law's home. I was still very jetlagged and confused by so many of the abrupt changes in my life. It was around noon, and my wife at the time suggested I go get some hamburgers for lunch. I got ready, went downstairs, and jumped in the car. As soon as I pulled out of the driveway, I was unsure where the nearest restaurant was, but I thought I would turn right and figure it out along the way. After driving for a while, I spotted a hamburger place. It gave me comfort to see some similarities between this restaurant and what I'd seen in Hollywood films. I felt like I was living the American Dream.

I decided to be bold and go through the drive-through for the first time, as we don't have these in Italy. As I drove up the path, I realized that I'd already passed the speaker. I backed up and got ready to order. I heard a voice that rather aggressively said, "Hello! What would you like to order today?"

I rehearsed in my head quickly, and then spoke. "Yes, hello, I would like a Big Mac, please."

The male voice replied, "I'm sorry, sir, but we do not make Big Macs here."

I thought that he'd misunderstood me due to my thick accent, so I repeated, "Yes, hello, I would like a Big Mac with French fries and ketchup."

I felt so proud of myself because it was the longest sentence I'd ever uttered in English.

The employee repeated, "I'm sorry, sir, this is Burger King, and we don't sell Big Macs here. Would you like a Whopper?"

Now I was getting very agitated and asked, "A Whopper? Is that a hamburger?"

"Yes, sir, it is a hamburger."

So I ended up ordering the Whopper for my wife and proceeded to pay. Then I started to think that maybe hamburgers were like pasta. In Italy, we don't have just one name for pasta. We have ziti, mostaccioli, spaghetti, linguini, but it's really all the same stuff. In America, I thought it must be the same. It must be the same hamburger with a different name, so I got the burger and then continued to drive.

I felt so happy about ordering food for the first time in a foreign country, and it made me feel so independent. In all this confusion, I'd forgotten to get a second hamburger for myself. Either way, I wanted to get more practice ordering, so I decided that I was going to get a sandwich next. Then I saw a sign for Subway. This time there wasn't a drive-through, so I parked the car and went inside. As soon as I walked in, I was greeted at the door. The employees were so friendly, and it was almost as if they knew I was coming. *Maybe the hamburger people told them*, I thought to myself.

I went to stand in line, and in front of me I noticed a large man with a beard. I decided to ask him how the ordering process worked. He looked me up and down as if I were an alien from Mars.

He said, "Can't you read the sign, man? It says: STEP 1: Pick bread. Just follow the steps."

I thanked him and started to read through all of the choices. Finally, it was my turn. I chose the bread, the meat, and the cheese. Then I was asked if I wanted any vegetables.

I jokingly replied, "Run it through the garden." The man put all the vegetables on the sandwich and somehow managed to close it.

On my way back home, my mind began to wander. All of a sudden, I began remembering this one shop in Florence that I would always visit. It was always rather dark inside, but you were often able to see the shadow of a man on the other side of the counter holding a big knife the size of a machete. In front of him was a massive mortadella, as large as a watermelon. He sliced the beast with a measured arm, and you could tell that it wasn't his first time attempting this. It was rather intimidating. Then I asked him if I could order a sandwich. He replied, "Sure, give me a moment. Go ahead and sit down." After ten minutes the man came out from behind the counter, placing a sandwich and an Orangina soda on my table. I didn't even have to ask what kind of bread, meat, or cheese I wanted. I took a bite of the sandwich and could feel the mortadella and the soft bread melting in my mouth. I felt like I was dreaming.

A few years later, I was speaking with my kids, and I told them about my first fast-food experience. Excitedly they asked me, "Daddy, which one was your favorite sandwich? Subway or the one at the shop in Florence?"

I replied, "Kids, come on. That isn't the point of the story. Obviously, the panino from the small shop in Florence was my favorite. My point is that in any circumstance, we have to adapt to our surroundings and do our best in any situation."

The Subway sandwich was great in Springfield, just as the panino was great in Florence, although I must confess, it was better. This brings me back to the small village in Poland. And now I'm wondering, *What kind of sandwich am I going to order?*

Philosophy

My father was a book collector. We had books everywhere around my house: in the study, in the living room, in the bedrooms, and in the garage. My mom was tired of dusting the bookshelves and told my dad to give some of the books away, but that didn't stop him from buying more. He would even give encyclopedia sellers some business. Their job probably wasn't easy. Decades ago, selling encyclopedias door-to-door was a last resort and a very unrewarding job. However, after a difficult month of very few customers, they could go to my dad's house to sell the updated version of their series. Many years later, unfortunately, my dad could no longer afford such luxuries and had to turn away these salespeople.

Today, my dad no longer buys books. He is eighty-six years old and has managed to buy a computer and slowly learn to download the most up-to-date information. The world has changed since my parents started their family. My four siblings and I needed to buy books when we started school. Most of them were used for one semester and then sold back, because we wanted to save as much pocket money as we could for going out on weekends. However, I remembered seeing a big case of books in the study downstairs, which had never been resold.

One day I opened the case and started reading the first book, a philosophy textbook that my brother had used in high school. The front page had a picture of the "thinking man" and Socrates, two eternal figures whose teachings have stayed close to my heart to this day. Looking at that front page ignited my senses but didn't give me the immediate curiosity to immerse myself in the subsequent pages. I felt a mix of reverence and fear.

It wasn't until many years later that I happily rediscovered philosophy, which promptly became a handy companion throughout my life's adventures. In ancient Greece, philosophy was the system of all knowledge and eventually branched out into astronomy, physics, politics, medicine, ethics, and logic. Philosophy cannot be clearly defined, even to this day, as there are many interpretations of it. In fact, there are as many definitions of philosophy as there are philosophers.

According to Socrates, philosophy involves asking questions about the world, because the unexamined life is not worth living. Aristotle proposed a more empirical approach to philosophy, dwelling on reason in an attempt to make things clear. Ultimately, all philosophers are in search of the true meaning of something, whatever that may be. While it's not guaranteed that they reach their goal in finding some truth about logic or ethics, they certainly enjoy the process of keeping themselves mentally occupied. With their brains at work—analyzing, speculating, and wondering—they demonstrate how to make use of, and appreciate, the gifts of intelligence and curiosity.

Philosophers may express opinions, but finding conclusive truths isn't an easy task. Even Jesus, standing in front of Pontius Pilate just before being condemned to the crucifixion, was asked the question: "What is the truth?" Jesus never answered that question directly. I believe that he knew the answer, or at least had an opinion about it, but he didn't want to alter this crucial moment. Most people would agree with Jesus that his father, God, is the ultimate truth. I will leave that question open for discussion, because when final answers are reached, there is no further room for discussion. What, then, would happen to philosophy, and all the debate that comes along with it?

Karl Marx had a more radical approach to thinking and once said, "Philosophers have only interpreted the world, in various ways; the point, however, is to change it." His attempt to change the world, although in good faith, led to the Communist Manifesto and the spread of socialism in Eastern Europe. Just thinking about ideas can be a good mental exercise, but putting them into action may yield unwanted results.

When I went to school, we often joked that philosophy is "the thing that, with or without, leaves everything unchanged." Basically, that's saying that philosophy is like a carousel that goes around and around, but nothing really happens. I don't think I had a personal perspective on philosophy until I moved to the United States. Sometimes it's necessary to step away from the usual routine of life and family (especially Italian families, who have such a stronghold on character and perception) and see things from another point of view.

When I first arrived in the US, I felt—or at least I imagined I felt—like an astronaut who'd moved to the moon. I saw Earth from afar: a round element suspended in space, slowly moving around the sun. I'd certainly never had this epiphany when I was sipping a cappuccino outside the café in my hometown. I began seeing reality with a new perspective and started to appreciate a philosophy of living that was new to me.

I remember the first time I drove down the streets of Springfield, Missouri. I couldn't believe that the people were taking turns at the intersections, knowing exactly when to pass, based on the assumption that each driver would be honest about who arrived first at the stop sign. Each car was moving along the intersection just fine, without issue. This system would never have worked in Italy; it would have been complete chaos. It's already a mess with traffic lights, and I couldn't imagine what would occur if crossing an intersection was based on the honesty of drivers.

When I moved into my apartment in Missouri, I barely knew my neighbors. Everyone was courteous, but they were very private about their lives. It was a nice change from Italy, where in my neighborhood, everyone knew everything about your family. Privacy was nonexistent in my town. Before leaving for America, I spent a year in a small town called Rignano sull'Arno, near Chianti. I lived in an apartment building close to my brother's. The apartment was on the second floor, and every day after work I would have to walk up many flights of stairs. By the time I reached the last step, the lady next door—a widow in her seventies—was already outside her door offering me some soup or other homemade dish she'd cooked.

From the window of my apartment, I could see people coming and going to buy bread from the bakery on the street below. Then, a group of teenagers would walk by, yelling, joking, and whistling to the cute girls they passed. Saturday mornings, I would walk to the plaza to buy a newspaper and meet with the locals and talk about work, family, and politics. Then I would get a cappuccino and a bombolone at the Café Feroci, stop by my brother's place, and go to the market for some groceries. By the time I returned home, I'd probably talked to most of the people in the town.

I should mention that when I spoke of the bombolone earlier, I didn't properly pause to describe this tasteful treat— the Italian version of a doughnut. I don't even know where to start, and my mouth is watering just thinking about these sweet, fluffy breads. Before I begin, you might ask me, what does this have to do with philosophy and lifestyle? Believe me when I say that there's plenty of philosophy in food, and a bombolone is no exception. It's made with flour, butter, sugar, and eggs. It is left to rise, and then shaped into a disklike form and fried in oil. The surface is covered in powdered sugar, and the inside is filled with a delicious cream with a consistency as soft as spongy cake. Think about it. How could you pass up such a dessert?

So, back to my story. Being in America was different in so many ways. After two years in Missouri, I moved to California and was staying in San Diego. I was missing the warmth of the people in my small village in Tuscany. At the same time, it was a nice change to be able to focus on myself, independent from my family, who had good intentions but often made me feel suffocated with attention. I certainly missed Rignano sull'Arno, but daily life in San Diego was so simple and nice. Everyone was so respectful and kind, and things ran smoothly and efficiently—so much so that I began questioning my Italian culture and thought that maybe the American way of life was the more intelligent approach to my existential dilemma. Productivity versus *la dolce vita* (the sweet life) seemed to work well.

Then, all of this punctuality and perfection began to lose its appeal. I started to miss my train in Italy that was always twenty minutes late, or the long line at the post office. I missed the loudness of the neighbors, the widow on the second floor, and of course, the bomboloni, which were made not by the hands of "productivity" but rather with the patience it took to make them soft and sweet pieces of heaven. I started to develop a theory: that there was an Italian philosophy and an American philosophy. The Italian philosophy consisted of dialogue, relationships, family, physical appearances, music, art, and the open expression of feelings. The American philosophy was made up of respect, straight lines, punctuality, honesty, and laws. I found myself praising the features in both the American and Italian philosophies, elucidating the merits of both cultures.

There are no fine lines of demarcation in philosophy. The yin and yang is closer to the reality of things than people may realize. I learned this through my friendship with Mark. I first met him during the summer at his house in Encinitas, a beach town north of San Diego. It was his wife's birthday party. As I entered the house, I could hear people talking in the living room across the hall. People were gathered around

Mark's wife, Josephine, who was in a wheelchair. She was in her late sixties, with long gray hair, green eyes, and rose-colored lips that brightened her face. When I met Josephine, she was still able to speak. Within two years, she'd become completely immobilized, and her body had shrunk to a mere one hundred pounds.

Mark was sitting next to the window, from which the lazy afternoon light was spreading across the floor. He greeted me with a smile. He knew I was coming, and my friend Paul, who'd invited me to this party, waved as I entered the room. I introduced myself to Mark, and he immediately asked me where I was from. I told him I was from a small town in Florence.

"I love Florence!" he responded enthusiastically. I wasn't surprised by his response because I'd been asked this question many times before. Those who would inquire about Italy would tell me about their vacations in Tuscany, and all the beautiful sites they visited. After our brief introduction, Mark presented me to Josephine. We spoke for a few minutes. She was still a beautiful woman, but I could tell that the illness was showing physical signs of deterioration. It was so ironic that she became ill. Throughout her entire life, she'd always eaten healthy foods, exercised, done yoga, and meditated. Mark, on the other hand, was a man of excess. He was overweight, ate fast food, and didn't exercise. The irony of life had put his wife in a wheelchair inching closer to death, while he was still breathing fine. This is another aspect of philosophy: sometimes logic and absurdity are equally present in life.

During the following years, I went to see Mark many times. The visits usually played out the same way every time: Josephine would be sitting on the couch watching television or would just stare blankly at the wall. Mark and I would talk for hours about everything in my life and his. He would explain to me how Josephine's unknown disease had rendered her motionless, and she eventually lost her ability to speak. Mark had his own way to communicate with her, though, and even a small movement of her eyes meant something, allowing Mark to tend to her needs. My conversations with Mark were quite philosophical and, honestly, how could they not be? Josephine was a constant reminder that life is very precious, and the illusion of being in control of our fate is indeed, just an illusion.

Mark would tell me, "It's mind over matter; if you don't mind, then it doesn't matter." There was some truth to the idea of letting go, to not take life too seriously, and take everything with a grain of salt. Mind over matter were the two faces of the same coin. Just like certainty and doubt.

"Life is like a school," Mark told me one afternoon, "but you never get a degree."

I frowned at his statement and responded, "Then what's the point of going to school if you don't get your diploma?"

Mark smiled and said, "The joy is not in the diploma, but in the lesson. It's just like hiking up a mountain. If the joy was at the top, the hikers would get there with a helicopter. Questions allow individuals to engage, to seek, and to explore. On the other hand, exclamations are the immovable certainty that can lead to fanaticism and violence. Think about how much blood has spilled over exclamations!"

I then asked, "Mark, are you saying that liberty, democracy, and respect for other people aren't values we should defend as the truth?"

Mark countered, "No, this is not what I mean. Indeed, the search for the truth, the questions we ask, should unite humanity over an endless respectful dialogue based on tolerance and liberty. Saint Augustine's famous quote was 'Love and do what you will.' This is a world of relativity; there isn't absolute good or bad. What you experience is not necessarily true, as your unique interpretation of the reality is based on your upbringing, language, culture, and many other experiences that have led you to this moment. You and I wear a pair of metaphorical glasses through which we see the world."

I was beginning to understand his ideas. I responded, "So, we live in a fictitious reality. The world as we see it is just our illusion, our interpretation of it. The perception of cappuccino is not based on a common interpretation but rather an individual perception."

Mark responded, "Indeed, the best cappuccino is the one that you make at home, because it is made with love. In fact, to paraphrase Saint Augustine again, 'Love is the answer.' He refers to love with a capital *L*, because it is not just any kind of love. Love is not about being good or following a specific path of redemption. Love is vivid passion. The love for a well-made cappuccino is love with a capital *L*."

I responded, "Of course it is, Mark."

Josephine passed away soon after. As she requested, she was cremated and placed in an urn that Mark kept in his bedroom. Sometimes I saw Mark talking to the urn, having deep conversations and arguments with it, as if Josephine were still alive.

Mark once told me, "A girl is going for the first time to La Scala, a famous theater in Milan, to see a concert. She's lost in the chaotic streets of the city. Then she sees a man with a violin walking by and asks him, 'How do I get to La Scala?' The man turns to her and responds, 'Practice, little girl. Practice.'"

So, in life, we may get lost at times, but all we must do is practice, practice. Socrates's efforts to examine the unexamined life is the effort to be aware, which can also be interpreted as practicing to die. In other words, philosophy can have a healthy dose of therapeutic effects in life, giving us some important tools to prepare ourselves for the moment when we will trespass into another dimension.

Where? How? Why? If we had the answer, how could we wonder? And how sweet it is to wonder, especially when accompanied by love, wine, and good food. Isn't that already the best of all possible worlds?

Yes, You Can

How many of you like to sing in the shower? I enjoy singing by myself, but not so much in public. I'm very self-conscious when it comes to performing in front of other people. Who knows, maybe I was born to be a talented singer, to be part of a band, or to be a tenor. Inside of me, however, there is fear, and I'm pretty sure I know where it comes from. I want to tell you a story from my childhood, but I'm not the main character. . . .

The protagonist is Paolo.

I was ten years old. My family went to church every Sunday, but the church we attended wasn't in our parish. My dad had a lot of friends at this other church an hour from our home, which in Italy is quite far just to go to a Sunday service. I loved this church, although I wasn't impressed by the forty-five-minute sermon I had to listen to. In fact, I couldn't wait for the Mass to be over and run out with all the children in the backyard of the church, playing soccer and hide-and-seek. Ah, that was my kind of heaven.

I had a special friend, Paolo. Every Sunday we would get together, and I remember chasing after lizards with him as well as following a tribe of ants to find out where their anthill was. Those are the fun things you do when you're ten, eleven, and twelve; and then suddenly, you're thirteen and then fourteen. Inside of us we start feeling that water, and then it starts boiling. Those are the hormones of a young

149

teenager. And everyone knows that when the water is boiling, it's time to throw the pasta in the pot. Suddenly, Paolo and my interests started shifting from lizards and ants to girls. Where were they? Most of them were part of the choir. Oh, what beautiful voices they had. So angelic!

Paolo and I made a decision. We needed, absolutely needed, to be a part of the choir. It didn't take long for us to figure out that the choir was meeting every Wednesday at such and such's home. On Wednesday, Paolo and I drove on our mini scooters to the location. We ran up the stairs; and a tall, robust man stopped us at the entrance of the house.

He asked, "Where are you going?"

"We came here to join the choir. It's our desire to become great singers," I replied. (Although in our heads, all that mattered was hearing those angelic voices.)

The man replied, "There's a fee to be paid. It's five dollars for the annual membership."

I responded, "No problem."

We paid our entrance fee and walked inside the house. We went down the stairs into a gorgeous room. Then, the most beautiful sight appeared before our eyes. The girls with the magical voices.

Hallelujah!

Paolo and I believed in heaven now. While we were enchanted by the girls who were gathering in their section of the room, the director of the choir approached us:

"Welcome, please sit down, and follow along as best you can."

Paolo and I sang the songs, really trying our best, and we ended up having so much fun. But at the end of the evening, the director called us over and said, "I'm very sorry, guys. Unfortunately, you're very bad singers, and I'm afraid you cannot be part of the choir. Here is your five dollars for the membership back!"

Paolo and I returned home very saddened. For me, that was the end of my career as a potential tenor. But not for Paolo.

He didn't give up. He convinced his parents to take him to rehearsal classes. Then he took private lessons. Meanwhile, he even learned how to play the guitar. One day when I went to Mass, he was there and was part of the choir, singing with so much contentment along with all the other singers, especially all the cute girls. (In fact, he later ended up marrying one of them.)

After coming to the United States, I eventually lost contact with Paolo. I know one thing for sure, though: he's still enjoying his singing and music. Now, you may look at me and tell me straight to my face: "What a quitter." Perhaps I am. Maybe those words are weighing upon me, and maybe my singing voice is somewhere waiting to be released so that I can unleash all my potential.

In life, you may encounter someone like the choir director. He may tell you not to bother, and that you weren't born with any special skills. Don't believe him. Keep going. Be brave, be bold, and trust in your potential. Remember Paolo. He persisted. Because the truth is that if you deeply desire something, you can accomplish it.

Yes, you can!

Guinness World Records

ᘓ

The Guinness World Records, like many other things, began with the purpose of settling an argument among people and to determine who the best was. After many disagreements, more people have started betting on what they claim to know or be able to do. The Guinness World Records have inspired people to accomplish extraordinary things; people who have had difficult childhoods or backgrounds have gone on to achieve amazing success. Whatever their final goal was, people believed in their strength, intelligence, and will. They were determined to triumph over any obstacle. It didn't matter if everyone told them it was impossible. It didn't matter how bizarre their goals might have seemed.

The most bizarre success stories in the Guinness World Records are sure to amaze you. For example, the largest bubblegum bubble ever blown (20 inches) or the most toilet seats broken by one's head in one minute (46 seats) or growing the world's heaviest onion (17 pounds).

Famous people are often mentioned in the Guinness World Records. This makes perfect sense, because they're part of the most elite group of gifted individuals. Michael Jackson's *Thriller* is the biggest-selling album of all time. Madonna is the top-selling female recording artist of all time. Roberto Benigni, who directed and starred in the film *Life is Beautiful*, holds the world record for the highest-grossing foreign-language film in North America.

However, not all records end up in the book or on the website. For some people, making records becomes a part of everyday life, and they don't bother inviting a crew to document their activities. They don't feel the need to be recognized in the official record of amazing accomplishments. For example, nobody has ever been curious to find out who holds the record for making the most homemade pasta sauce. But I know that the record exists. I know the individual who has made it possible. In fact, that person is my father.

Every year during tomato season, my dad goes to the local market to buy massive quantities of tomatoes for the sauce. The final taste varies every year, depending on the quality of the ingredients. Last year he made eighty pounds of tomato sauce and forty pounds of pesto, all sealed in glass jars and stored for the rest of the year. Some of the jars are given to friends and family. The last time I went to visit him, I had pesto almost every time I went to his house. He'd made four kinds of pesto, and he wanted me to taste all of them before I left for America. He also insisted that I take some jars home with me and tried to put some in my suitcase. The jars weighed a total of seventeen pounds and took up most of the room in my luggage. I believe that my suitcase would have been the record holder for the most jars of pesto sauce taken overseas.

Luckily, my sister helped me and offered to take some of the jars. Can you imagine if customs had opened my suitcase to inspect it at the airport? I might have been on the news, labeled as the Italian who tried to smuggle seventeen pounds of pure, unrefined homemade pesto and tomato sauce into the US.

Indeed, whether they're official or not, records are amazing, especially for those people who make such an effort to make the impossible a reality. My dad is no exception.

Swordfish

esus's first disciples were fishermen. The sign of the fish is symbolic in Christianity. My father enjoyed fishing, partly for his religious beliefs. Once a month, he used to go with several friends to the ocean and fish all night. The following weekend, a dinner would follow with family and friends. We would all meet at the home of one of the families from church. Sometimes the crowd of people could even reach a hundred people. These gatherings were fun occasions where my father and his friends could tell stories about their fishing adventures.

One night my father recounted a story of this swordfish they'd attempted to catch, but they weren't able to bring it home. He'd promised that the next dinner was going to be one based on swordfish because he was sure he was going to catch one. So, the next month, he and his friends went back to the ocean, this time looking for swordfish. They tried really hard, but the swordfish were smarter than they were, and they came home empty-handed. What were they to do? Their promise had to be kept, and the dinner still needed to be served. My father wasn't one to get discouraged. He went to the fish market, talked to the right people, and shortly thereafter, he was sold a huge swordfish for the dinner. My father and his friends also took pictures with the head of the swordfish.

The dinner was a success, and everybody was happy. Eventually, my father confessed to me what really happened. I was a small child, but I still couldn't believe it.

"Dad," I asked, incredulously, "you lied to us?"

My father responded, "Son, do you remember that night? We didn't brag about our fishing skills. We just made sure that everybody had fun and had enough to eat. Did you have fun?"

"Yes," I replied.

He said, "Then what does it matter if we caught the fish or if we bought it? Doesn't the fact that everybody had a good time matter more?"

I reluctantly replied, "I guess."

My dad was right. Sometimes we get so fixated on our ideas. This story made me think about how everything is relative. Did they catch the fish or buy the fish? It really doesn't matter, as long as they brought *back* the fish. And if it doesn't matter, who cares what happened?

The Chef

My dad taught me that a small lie is acceptable when the benefits outweigh the consequences. However, my friend Bobby is the perfect example of how an unjustified lie is like a clogged sink. In Tuscany, we say that "the devil makes the pots but not the covers." Meaning that what is planned in bad faith is always incomplete. Just as a pot without a cover will eventually make the soup spill out, a lie will eventually let the truth come out. Bobby did boil some soup without the cover. . . .

One day Bobby was running on the treadmill and looking at the people coming and going through the entrance of the gym. Then he saw his trainer, Kristen, leaving her office. He waved at her, and she walked toward the treadmill.

"Hi, how are you doing?" Kristen asked Bobby, who was sweating and gasping for air.

"I'm doing great! Thank you, Kristen. I love the workout schedule you made me."

"My pleasure. If you don't know how to do some of the exercises, let me know. I can help you."

"Sure. I may need you to slap my hand if you see me wandering toward the vending machine."

"I don't think I included that on the workout schedule."

"I know, but the temptation of having that chocolate bar makes me crazy!"

Bobby looked at her finger. Kristen didn't have a wedding ring. He felt bold and asked, "We should go out sometime."

"Bobby, I'm married."

"Oh, sorry. I didn't see a ring . . ."

"I know. I don't wear it all the time. I thought I saw you come in with your girlfriend . . ."

"Ex-girlfriend. We broke up."

"Sorry to hear that. How did you break up?"

"She left me. The night before, she told me that she loved me; and the day after, she said she was done. It wasn't easy. After a week of listening to Michael Bolton songs, I called her and told her that I'd throw myself under a train. And she texted me the Amtrak schedule. . . ."

"It doesn't surprise me. Women are tough! Don't ever underestimate a woman. How are you doing now?"

"Well, I keep myself busy. I decided to get a second job. I work my regular job during the day, and then at night I work at a restaurant."

"What kind of cuisine? Asian fusion?"

"Kristen, come on . . . what's fusion? It's an Italian restaurant. What else could it be?"

"My favorite. There's some fusion in Italian food too."

"I guess! Tomatoes are Mexican, and spaghetti is Chinese . . . and Alfredo sauce is American. It's definitely fusion. . . .

"Ha ha. My friend and I could come and visit you. She is single and very cute. You'd like her. It would be a good idea for you guys to meet."

"That would be fantastic. I'll give you my number on my way out as well as the address of the restaurant. What's your friend's name?"

"Holly. We can come on Wednesday. Are you going to be there?"

"Wednesday sounds great. We serve zabaglione dessert on Wednesday."

"Is 7:00 good?"

"Perfect."

"What do you do at the restaurant?"

"I am . . . the chef."

"No kidding. Wow. I can't wait to tell my girlfriend. I must go. Please, leave your number with the receptionist. I'll call you to confirm. Ciao!"

Bobby was inviting Kristen and her friend to the restaurant where he was . . . the dishwasher, not the chef. He'd gotten a job at the restaurant to get over his ex-girlfriend, and the only job he was qualified for was dishwasher. It certainly didn't sound as intriguing to say that he was a dishwasher, but he could have just been honest about it. It was much more colorful to make his friends think that he could chop eggplant and sauté zucchini. Wednesday was just a few days away and certainly wasn't enough time to learn how to cook seafood risotto and veal piccata. Bobby had to find a solution—and quick.

Bobby involved the entire staff to make his lie stand. He started with the chef, the real one, Pantaleone, who was willing to cooperate but didn't seem to grasp all the fuss behind Bobby's special date.

"Why did you have to make it so complicated? To impress a woman? She's going to find out anyhow. Never underestimate a woman."

"That's funny. That's exactly what Kristen told me about my ex. Never underestimate a woman."

"But you keep insisting on it. I would have made this very simple."

"Yes. How?"

"It's about taking it out."

"Taking what out?"

"The plumber."

"What plumber?"

"Women don't care about you being a chef or a dishwasher . . . but they care about the plumber . . . that makes a huge difference."

"What are you talking about? The plumber?"

"*Your* plumber."

"I don't take out the plumber randomly. Before I do any plumbing, I knock at the door."

"At the end of the night, if she finds out the truth, her radiator may not be too hot for you. Why did you make it so complicated? Man! And don't forget that you owe me a bottle of Jack Daniels. All this show to make your lady believe that you are me, when if you were me, you would be a plumber, not a chef. And I would be all over her radiator."

"Thank you, chef, pardon . . . plumber. I owe you one."

The hostess had been ordered to alert the kitchen when Kristen and Holly arrived at the restaurant. Bobby was going to put on Pantaleone's apron and greet his friends. The owner of the restaurant knew about Bobby's mad adventure and had agreed to go along with his plan if he didn't disturb the other customers. It was on!

Bobby was alerted that the guests had arrived. He went into the dining room. Kristen and Holly were sitting at the table while the waiter, Tony, was describing the wine list.

Kristen saw Bobby, "Hi, Bobby! The restaurant is beautiful. Come give me a hug."

"Good evening."

"Oh, and this is my friend Holly," Kristen said, directing the palm of her hand toward her friend.

"Nice to meet you, Bobby. I was just reading the menu. It looks amazing," Holly said with a smile.

"Thank you. Tony, don't forget to tell them about the dessert special, the zabaglione . . . we make it fresh. I must go back in the kitchen. See you later. It's a busy night. Make yourself comfortable. Enjoy."

Kisses and hugs followed, and then Bobby went back into the kitchen. After changing clothes, he went back to washing and drying the pots and pans.

"So . . . what am I cooking for these ladies, on your behalf?" asked Pantaleone.

"I don't know," replied Bobby, "but it better be good. My reputation as a chef is in your hands."

"Man, you'd be better off confessing."

Tony came into the kitchen. "Here's the order. Oh my! That Holly looks pretty hot."

"Hey, slow down. Why do you think I'm working so hard?"

"Are you? I thought that *we* were the ones working hard for you!"

"What do you care? Don't you have a girlfriend?"

"Yes, but we aren't talking right now."

"Come on, you guys are always going back and forth."

"What can I say? We break up; then she shows up at my door, and we inevitably have sex."

"That doesn't sound too bad. Never underestimate a woman . . . they know what they want."

"What? Have you turned into a wise man now? How about you use some of that wisdom in becoming a chef?"

"And why would I want to do that when, according to Pantaleone, you just need to be a good plumber?"

"What are you talking about? What plumber?" said Tony.

"I think I need to give both of you some lessons on how to deal with women," said Pantaleone.

Everything seemed to go smoothly. Kristen and Holly were enjoying their meal and couldn't contain their euphoria. I was told once by a woman friend that the secret to a successful date is a dinner that includes a combination of pasta, dessert, and wine. It's undeniable that the way to a man's heart is through his stomach, and the same can be said for a woman. Preparing food for a woman is a tool of seduction that a man can utilize. The elapsed time between the preparation of the food and the consummation of the relationship adds more flavor to their passionate love. Lucky chefs! And lucky Bobby, who had Holly fantasizing over him while she was eating fettuccini Bolognese and sipping Sangiovese wine.

Two young and good-looking gentlemen arrived at the restaurant and sat at the table next to Holly and Kristen and began a conversation with them. "Looks like you ordered fettuccine Bolognese. A simple dish but one of my favorites," said one the guys. "I love the cuisine here. Chef Pantaleone is amazing."

"You mean Bobby," said Holly.

"Bobby? Bobby who?" asked the gentleman.

"Bobby the chef. We know him. He's our Italian friend."

"We may not be talking about the same person. The chef is Pantaleone."

"Pantaleone?"

"I think the Bobby you're talking about is the new dishwasher. We're regulars here; we'd know if he was the chef."

"I can't believe Bobby lied to us."

"I don't think your friend had bad intentions; he just doesn't know to never underestimate a woman. . . ."

Bobby was no longer the pop-star chef he'd aspired to be, but rather a pots-and-pans-silly-pants. The effort to create an illusion backfired. Lying in bad faith is like boiling soup in pots without covers, which eventually lets the truth spill out. Bobby had learned a lesson. *I* had learned a lesson too, as I was he—Bobby the phony chef!

The Boss

𝕏

A mother was sitting in the kitchen. It was just past one o'clock in the morning, and she was reading a magazine while nervously scratching her head. Her eighteen-year-old son had gone out with his friends and hadn't come home. This wasn't the first time he'd acted this way. He was quite inconsiderate and thought that his parents' insistence on a curfew was irrational. He always claimed that his buddies didn't have the same restrictions, and that it wasn't his fault if his friends always arrived late to the club, thus lengthening his time there. Suddenly the door opened. The boy closed the door behind him and turned on the light in the hall.

"Do you see what time it is?" the mother angrily asked. "Where were you? Late again. Your father went to sleep, but tomorrow you'll hear it from him too."

"Mom, you know how it is. What do you want me to do? Leave the club when people start arriving? You understand, don't you? It's two in the morning. I actually think I got home pretty early."

"Early? We were so worried, and you don't seem to care."

"Seriously, Mom, do we have to have this conversation right now? If you want to be worried, then that's fine with me. I have friends to hang out with, and a life to live."

"You won't have a life when I take your car keys away."

"Well, then, I'll have my friends come and pick me up."

"No, because you're going to stay home."

"Mom, who do you think you are? Are you my boss? I can't wait to move out of this house so that I can finally make my own decisions. No more bosses in my life."

"Sure, son, good luck with that. You really think you won't have to answer to other people for the rest of your life?"

"Okay, I'll have a boss when I get a job, but at least she won't be waiting for me to come back home from the club at two in the morning."

"No, my son. That's not the boss I'm speaking of."

"Oh yeah? Which boss, then? The priest of the church?"

"No."

"Then who?"

"I'm talking about a boss that we all have."

"Okay, I see where this conversation is going. Jesus is my boss, and now I'm probably going to hell, right? Or is it the Pope?"

"No. The boss I speak of is a gentleman called Time."

"Okay, Mom. I'm going to bed. I'm not in the mood to get philosophical right now."

"Go on to bed, then."

The son went to his room. However, he wasn't able to fall asleep. He kept thinking about the last remark his mother had made: Time is a boss, and a nice one, because she'd described him as a gentleman. What could she have meant? The boy was finally able to sleep. He awoke and found himself in the middle of nowhere. He jumped up from his bed and started walking. He was walking on air, just like an astronaut suspended in space. Floating around him were various clocks that were all running at different times.

"Is anybody out there?" he asked. All was quiet.

Then he heard someone reply, "Welcome."

"Who is that? Where are you?"

"Hello, I am Time."

"Time?"

"Yes, I am your boss."

"Show yourself! Where am I? Take me back home!"

"You cannot make such demands. I am your boss."

"I don't care! Just take me back to my mom! Please!"

"Oh, now you want your mom. Well, I'm not sure if you'll get back home."

"Who do you think you are? Come out here so I can kick your ass! Let me see your face!"

"I don't have a face. I am Time."

"Sure, man, and as long as we're lying, go ahead and call me the president."

"Welcome. I have a few questions for you and would like you to cooperate."

"Why would I do that?"

"I guess you don't have to. I won't be able to make much use of your time."

"Okay, what's your question?"

"If time was money, what would you buy with it?"

"The first thing that comes to mind is to buy more time."

"And then what?"

"I'm not sure."

"You see, every time you're not sure, you're depleting your investment. You don't need more time. You just need to use it better."

"How?"

"Give it a purpose."

"Every second?"

"Pretty much."

"But I'm not always in control of my time. People are always telling me what to do."

"You control your actions, but I'm still your boss. Use time to your advantage. Give purpose to what you do, and life will bring you joy."

"So that means that I can't have any fun? Am I predestined to just run around like a madman?"

"No, absolutely not. However, you should use your time wisely. Are you giving your time a purpose? Ask yourself this question, and act accordingly. How about coming home at two in the morning and making your mother worried? Is that time well spent? Is that giving you a purpose?"

"Every second has to have a purpose? That sounds very stressful."

"Well, sure. You'll be stressed out at the beginning because you've never treasured the value of time. It will take time to learn. But as you learn to act with purpose, even hanging out with friends will contribute to your life. However, I'm still your boss, and I get to determine how long your experience on Earth will last."

"And then what?"

"You'll see. One day, you will see. One day, I will become your illusion."

"You can exist and be an illusion?"

"Yes, I exist, and at the same time, I don't. I am timeless."

"If you're timeless, how can you be my boss?"

"As long as you're a human being living on this Earth, you're subject to the time between birth and death. Now that I've enlightened you, you may go back to sleep."

The boy woke up the next morning, realizing that it had all been a dream. He went to the kitchen where his mother was preparing breakfast.

"Good morning, son."

"Good morning, Mom. I'm sorry for last night."

"Son, I just want you to know that I love you and care about you. And I only speak in your best interests."

"I know, Mom. You know what happened last night? I talked to my boss."

"Time?"

"Yes!"

"What did he tell you?"

"He told me many things, but the most important of all was to give you a kiss and tell you how much I appreciate you. I love you, Mom."

"I love you too, son."

Part II

Carnival of Poems

Missing You

From the top of the hill,
I observe you half-asleep,
Lazily and cozily stretched
On your bed of country fields,
Covered in a blanket of mist,
Glittering of night lights
Under a summer-gray dark sky.

Today, I went to see you,
I strolled down your busy streets,
Marveling at your mature skin
Bathed along by the Arno river.
You have become a splendor,
A display of human genius
That your people shaped with glory.

The vein underneath your grounds
Pulse of everlasting warm blood
Drenched of indelible memories,
Of poets rhyming in your gardens,
Of painters chanting you in pictures,
Of sculptors sawing you with marble,
Of builders that a dome erected for your crown.

I feel intensely bound to you,
Familiar with your unique ways,

The Tuscan Who Sold His Fiat to the Pope

Rooted in thinking and learning,
Guardian of humankind's progress,
While youthful and burlesque,
You adopt what makes you wise
To remind us that life is also a time to play.

I keep looking at your beauty
That you reveal with generosity.
I want you so much more now
That I live from you apart and
Come to see you for a short while.
Indeed, it's never quite enough
'Cause I miss you as soon as I depart.

Bye, bye, Florence, I must leave you now.
I am going back to America,
But I will always carry you in me.
Next year, I will come back,
Cuddled again in your motherly chest,
Because you are my Town,
The one that I will never forget.

One of a Country

One day, God woke up,
Resolute to have some fun.
He made all sorts of stuff,
He worked nonstop, around the clock,
Without even taking breaks for lunch,
Never being satisfied enough.

Constellations, stars, planets,
Solar system, Jupiter, Venus,
And then the best of all,
The project most ambitious,
He gave birth to a blue orb
That He called Planet Earth.

First the sky was placed on top,
A protecting celestial volt,
Like a glass dome,
To filter the sunlight waves,
To make lightning and rainbows,
Snow, sunrises, and sunsets.

God splashed Earth with oceans,
Inhabiting it with creatures,
Fish, amphibians, mammals,
He constructed durable ground

The Tuscan Who Sold His Fiat to the Pope

With plants, trees, flowers, and then,
For a final touch: men and women.

He looked at his last creation,
A spectacular vision,
Original and unmatched,
A chest full of colors and flavors,
A logical but chaotic realization,
A cozy corner of the Universe.

But as he observed the Blue Planet,
One more thing was missing.
He decided to play some more,
Carving the earth, creating a peninsula,
Mixing the very best of the elements,
And gave this landmass the name . . . Italy.

The glimmer of his final creature
Caused envy in all human beings,
Who felt unjustly treated
Because they didn't get to have
So many amenities and beauties,
As their countries were not comparable to Italy.

She was immaculate like a queen,
Crowned with the snowy Alps,
The Apennines curving her body,
Immersed in the Mediterranean Sea,
With pearls like Florence and Rome,
And the lakes of Como and Maggiore.

God listened to the French, the Dutch,
The Americans, and the Spanish,
Not to mention the most upset,
The Germans, who threatened a war
If the situation was not alleviated,
Correcting the inequality with Italy.

Finally, God turned to the humans,
And with an authoritarian voice said:
"You don't have to worry,
I am God, after all.
Thus, to make things right among you,
I will place a new species in Italy.

Of people who speak their minds,
Who don't obey traffic lights,
Who eat Nutella instead of peanut butter,
Cornettoes and cappuccinos for breakfast,
Who don't respect personal space,
To whom I will give the name . . . Italians."

It was in this way that the almighty God
Put to rest the protests of other countries
Who were not content with the status quo,
Giving them reason to envy Italy,
God making preferences in His creation,
On the sixth day from its initiation.

Any story related to the Genesis
Will have a note at the very bottom
That explains what really happened
In the first week of the creation,
When God had to invent Italians
To make up for the beauty of their land.

The Italians are aware of what occurred,
But they don't mind the gossips.
They continue to enjoy themselves,
Immersed in the sun of plenty,
Driving Ducati, Ferrari, and Fiat,
Drinking wine and eating pasta,
Kissing in the streets of their cities
As if any day could be their last.

The Tuscan Who Sold His Fiat to the Pope

They have their priorities,
And for anything that doesn't really matter,
They wait until tomorrow.
Because today is today,
They don't feel any reason to be sorry.
Why would they?
The calamari is ready,
The dinner is served.
Let's pray to God
For being so generous with Italians
And making then one of a kind,
Of making Italy one of a country!

One of a Country
–Part Two

I know a country in this world
That can be terrible and terrific.
Therefore, my question is:
Will I start with the good news?
And then get to the bad?
Or the other way around?
Even though, I got to thinking,
In the end, it will not matter,
As this country will continue to have
Its problems as well as its merits.

You may have already guessed
The name of this nation,
One that you surely have heard of.
It's in Italy, and only there
Will you find three volcanos,
Etna, Stromboli, and Vesuvius,
The Alps and the Mont Blanc,
Lakes of Como and Garda,
Sicily, Sardinia, and Cinqueterra,
All nicely shaped like a boot.

It's a country with great history,
Of ancient stones and ruins

That date back to the Romans,
To its first King, Romulus.
But even before his reign,
To the people called Etruscans,
Maybe the ancestors of the Celtics,
Without forgetting the Greeks,
Fathers of wisdom and learning,
Influencers of Italy from the onset.

Alas, since the time of Rome,
Italy was full of contradictions,
Of unity and diversity,
Of efficiency and disorganization,
Of splendor and decadence,
Which at times has made
Government a corrupt word,
Tax evasion a national sport,
And public transportation delayed
Even without the union strikes.

Italy is proud of its ancient beauty
As well as its modern charm.
It is the homeland of Ferrari,
Lamborghini, and Alfa Romeo,
Motorcycles named Guzzi and Ducati.
Few can compete with Italians
In matters of design and style,
As they are founders of fashion,
Of famous ateliers such as Armani,
Valentino, Dolce and Gabbana.

While Italians sing along,
Allegro, andante, and *adagio,*
With Caruso and Pavarotti,
At La Scala in Milan,
They make life resemble

Operettas or plain dramas
Because they wear their hearts
On their sleeves without shame
If they feel the need to cry or laugh.

To conclude, let's not forget
That it's time to eat.
Let's all sit down and cheer
To the good and the bad,
To the uniqueness of Italy.
Make sure to bring something to share.
Pasta and marinara sauce,
Lasagna and chicken piccata,
Gelato, cannoli, and tiramisu.
Let's thank God for making Italy
One of a kind, one of a country,
Such a fantastic destination
For visitors from all over the world.

Let's celebrate today,
Because tomorrow is another day,
Tomorrow, nobody knows.
Today is the day to be happy.
Amen, cheers, *mangia*,
and *Buon Appetito*!

The Water Spring of the Tuscan Apennines

At our house we eat good food,
Simple dishes made from scratch.
We drink fine red wine
And the pure water from the spring,

Bottled by us at the source,
At the forest of Usignolo
Where I went with my family
To get the county's best water.

My mother caringly prepared
A generous basket for the picnic
With bread, cheese, and salami,
Fruits, nuts, and a few pieces of pie.

My father loaded the car
With bottles, big and small,
Jars and all sorts of flasks,
To get fresh water from the spring.

To reach Mount Badalone,
It took us about an hour.
It sits on the Tuscan Apennines
Just on the way past Pistoia.

The Tuscan Who Sold His Fiat to the Pope

I was so excited and happy
To spend those afternoons
Outdoors during the summer,
When at home the weather was sticky hot.

Up on those green mountains,
We walked under the acacias
And along the small creek
In the most absolute quiet and peace.

Sometimes the pebbly road
Would get busy with local people,
Who came to walk in the green pastures
And get some refreshments to bring home.

At the spring were two benches
On which people sat to chit-chat
While the kids were running around
Under the shadows of the trees.

We were truly experts of the place,
And so, we found a little corner
Secretly hidden from the path
Where we ate on the grass.

I do not know what the reason was,
Why I had such a big appetite:
Maybe the fine air or the running?
But I would always finish the leftovers.

And what could have been better
Than drinking the pure water,
Just taken at the source,
So refreshing, tasty, and clear?

Then, from who knows where,
One could hear the nightingale,

With his unique chirping,
Harmoniously filling the valley.

His singing would combine
With the gurgling of the creek,
With the swish of the trees,
And the eager flying bees.

The nightingale kept us attentive,
Just like we were at La Scala
Listening to a great tenor
Or one of Verdi's operas.

Then the dusk came down in the forest.
We gathered all our things,
Jumped back in the car,
Rich with our precious harvest of water.

Our provisions were plenty for a month.
The crystal water of the spring
Would always be on the table,
Not only to quench thirst,

But as a symbol to our family
Of those afternoons spent together,
Laughing, running, and joking,
Jovial, carefree, and happy.

Life of an Accountant

They call us bean counters.
We are the ones who sort out numbers,
The true and brave error hunters
Behind skyscrapers of papers.

Our days start at eight in the morning.
We are sharp, exact, like the Swiss.
We park our cars, run in the office,
And clock in without making a hiss.

The in-box is full of questions
The company demands to know,
If we are making any money,
Or the owner will surely show.

It's time to get the work done,
To run numbers in the system,
Create financial statements,
Balance sheets and rent rolls.

No need to wait a second more,
Let's book that journal entry,
It will make the books look good,
Increase the revenue by a penny.

The Tuscan Who Sold His Fiat to the Pope

Relax, there's no need to panic,
We are the number ghostbusters.
We won't let any issue beat us
Even when the odds are against us.

Every day is a new adventure
To find a needle in the haystack,
To run reports for the joint venture,
Or to make a big deposit in the bank.

Whoever said that accounting
Is one of the safest jobs to have,
When we are running around the office,
Madly like spinning tops!

And let's not talk about tax season.
We can't even go to the bathroom,
We are so busy for some reason,
As if the office turned into an ER.

We don't suffer from depression
But at times may feel "depreciation."
We may not be completely in balance
When desiring higher compensation.

When it's five, we go home,
Satisfied with our crunching efforts.
We go to bed with a smile,
Counting sheep as we fall fast asleep.

These are the trials of an accountant,
But we accept them with pride.
Despite being seen as awfully boring,
We are indeed busy bees,
Because we have a mission:
To save the world with numbers,
Our quest, quite demanding,

To deduce what is out of balance,
Bringing some sense (or at least we think)
To this planet that is such a mess.

Therapy

One Sunday, I was at the square,
Sipping an espresso by the coffee shop,
Catching up with some friends,
When the bell rang at one o'clock.

The barber, Signor Guido Labarba,
A man of intellect and philosophy,
Asked me if I had seen in the paper,
The article about "Therapy."

I didn't know of such a concept,
Since I tried to stay away from the gossip.
There are so many "ideas,"
It feels just like walking inside an Ikea.

But this theory sounded fun,
And since we were hanging out,
I asked him if he had a minute to spare,
Just in case I needed to be aware.

Guido Labarba started gesturing,
Attesting to the soundness of the idea,
Which explained many things,
Including those that seemed so weird.

He explained that humanity is a big caravan
Of people who share the same purpose,

The Tuscan Who Sold His Fiat to the Pope

Who must make good use of their time,
Given to them in this dream of nonsense.

Some have a great passion for sports,
Some for the sciences or literature,
Some for the sacred or the hedonistic,
Or any art, ancient or futuristic.

Indeed, we, the inhabitants of this world,
Embark on some mission or passion,
And really, it doesn't matter what it is
If it relieves the pain within.

The theory wants only to prove
That men are better being busy,
Giving or trying to make some sense
Of a place where logic is quite latent.

Because, let's be frank:
This world is a hospital full of patients
With a disease that is widespread,
To be exact, of being sick in the head.

We dwell in an authentic madhouse,
So perfectly crazy that one may wonder
If the inventor did this on purpose
To laugh himself deliriously to death.

Therefore, it doesn't matter what you do
To keep the wolf from the door,
So just choose the therapy that fits you best
Without harming your fellow friends.

Nobody will ever leave alive
From this tragicomic place.
Hence, you better think about that:
Why make such a big fuss?

Therapy

It was with such fervor,
That Guido explained to me
The theory of Therapy,
Of which he had found a cure.

With the same fervor I will say the same:
Do whatever you want, however you like,
As long as the therapy gives you some peace,
And respect for your fellow friends.

Nobody knows if tomorrow will come,
But let's just deal with today.
Let's make the best or our lives
Without having to go astray.

This is a dream, after all,
An illusion hard to understand.
A little bit of therapy
Is the best recipe for us all,
Clueless inhabitants
Of this sanatorium of ours!

The Holy Grail

The English language
Has so many uses for "holy"
I have lost count of how many:
Holy cow,
Holy smokes,
Holy crap,
Holy moly,
Holy Mike,
Holy guacamole,
And on and on,
Because holy is everywhere,
Even my pet is a holy cat!
But what about the Holy Grail?
Why so much secrecy
About this holy relic,
The most desired cup,
With unlimited powers
To please readily
Our most recondite aspirations,
The holy as well as
Those not so holy?
And what if the Holy Grail
Wasn't anything other than
That which is wholly holy,
That which is ourselves,
That which we must

Hold
And love.
Because to love ourselves,
Is to love all,
Holy and unholy?
Wouldn't that be
A holy cool idea?
Holy, holy wow!
It would be just as holy as
Living holy on a holly,
The holy of holies!

Lottery

5, 8, 17, 30, 48,
These are the winning numbers
Given to me by the whisper
Of the goddess Bonanza
In a dream while I slept.

I have no doubt
That this numerical series
Will make me filthy rich.
I can pay old and new bills
And change my life in a second.

On Saturday, it's the drawing,
On Sunday, I will laugh,
On Monday, I will make that call
To inform my boss
Of some news I need to share.

"I'm sorry for the late notice,
But I have an urgent request,
To use all my time off.
I will submit my time sheet
For instant approval.

I am leaving tomorrow
For a trip around the world,

And stop at a remote island.
I'm not sure when I'll get back.
Would you please hire a temp?

Oh, and on that island,
They don't have a clue
About laptops or spreadsheets,
I am sorry to inform you,
Remote logging in won't be an option."

Thank you, numbers, for setting me free.
I have no obligations of any sort,
No need to set the alarm in the morning.
I can journey like Columbus
And explore the seven seas.

With millions in my wallet,
I can buy the latest sports car,
A mansion with twelve bathrooms,
Season passes to see the Lakers,
Coach my team and win the Super Bowl.

I have money for my big family,
Enough to share with the IRS,
And to buy my lovely honey
The most expensive diamond
And the rarest of flowers.

Saturday is here already.
I shouldn't need to check the numbers.
Should it be just a formality
Because I have already won.
The goddess Bonanza said so.

Here are my five numbers.
What the heck! What happened!
I got one to match but not the rest.

Lottery

What to do with all my dreams
To go free and sail around the world?

But nothing is lost,
I will not despair.
Here are my new lucky five
That I dreamed of last night.
I will play them on Friday.

I am not the kind to give up
As long as I keep trying,
I will always have a chance
To win the ambitious prize,
Fill my pockets with gold and green.

But then, if I think better,
Seriously, what do I care?
Haven't I already won
The best girlfriend
That no lottery
Could ever match . . . ?

(I must confess. The last stanza increased my "credit
score" with my girlfriend, which is valuable to
have with a woman. After all, for a man, it's all
about earning points in order to win her heart.)

Ode to a Pisolino

A *pisolino* every day,
Meaning afternoon nap,
Keeps the headaches away.
Indeed, my amore and I think
This is how one stays fit,
Recharging the mind
And keeping the body strong.
Thumbs up for a nap.
Yes, I am for a *pisolino*,
You and I hugging together
Under the covers of our bed.
It's time to shut the curtains,
To deflect the sunlight from the wall,
And breathe in the lazy air of the room.
It's time for an afternoon nap.
Close your eyes . . .
And sleep until two,
Zzzzzzzzzzzzzzzzzz.

Facebook

After several postings, likes, and emojis,
Contemplating how to make more friends,
Descartes would have ultimately concluded:
"I have a Facebook profile; therefore, I exist."
Thinking is no longer part of the equation.
Posting is what matters, every day,
Give timely reports of daily activities,
Especially those with zero relativity.

"What's on your mind?"
Compelling, Facebook provokes you
To share with the social crowd
Something elaborated by the mind.
But, alas, how can you create
Anything out of your mind
When just spending time on Facebook
Seems to have no rational *cogito*?

Maybe Facebook meant:
"Do you still have anything in your mind?"
Because if so,
It's better you empty it right away
And get ready to fill your head
With all sorts of nonsense,
Including sharing pictures
Of you sitting on the toilet.

The Tuscan Who Sold His Fiat to the Pope

We have entered a new era
Of self-obsessed, compulsive people
Who have invaded our society
With its waves of annoying vanity.
"Facecrack" gives us an all-new high,
With its euphoric effects
That offer our "ego" no doubt
That we exist and matter.

Maybe, Facebook is another way
To flee from the light inside of us,
That potential that we fear most.
The idea is to make us believe
That what's out there matters more
Than to have our own experiences,
To feel light instead of spotlight,
That light inside of us,
That ubiquitous consciousness
That's waiting to radiate
In ourselves more than anywhere else.

Summertime in Carlsbad, California

Oh, how I love the summer,
A time for freedom and bathing suits,
barbecue and food on the go,
By the beach chilling with some booze.

On the sidewalks of Carlsbad,
I see a hectic parade of colors,
Like an overflowing bazaar
Mixing together under the sun.

The ocean waves impatiently
Inviting all the people into the water,
To run and dance with joy
With the crabs and the seagulls.

Surfers champion the waves
While pretty girls chat on the sand,
And guys suck in their beer bellies,
Hoping to look sexy to the ladies.

But who is that man in the ocean?
Oh my, look at that boiling water.
He must have done a big fart
That made all the fish dart.

The Tuscan Who Sold His Fiat to the Pope

And who is that curvy lady?
She sure made a big effort
To fit in that tiny swimsuit,
But at least her goggles fit her perfectly!

What a crazy day in Carlsbad!
What a bountiful variety.
People of any kind in clothes of any brand,
Who come here to sit in the sand.

Biking and smiling on my way home,
This sunny day in the warm summer,
I cannot wait to have that beer.
I'm glad I made my home right here.
HAPPY SUMMERTIME!

So Many Rules

I'm so confused
By so many rules!
Everywhere I go,
There's no room
To be free, unless
One wants to seem weird.

Rules of every kind
That come from all over.
While you may wonder
And scratch your head,
You need to know
Or you'll feel like an outcast.

The human's wild mind
Has an ability to limit things,
Giving specifics on what is "normal,"
How to do all kinds of things,
Although, from Alaska to Jamaica,
It can mean nine hundred things.

Indeed, some of the rules
You'll have fun discovering,
While traveling around the world,
Because every country
Has its own definition

The Tuscan Who Sold His Fiat to the Pope

Of who is a fool.

Please, have some manners,
And eat tacos with your hands,
But only if you're in Mexico.
In the Middle East,
Eat pita bread with your left hand.
In Italy, use a fork and knife for pizza.

I would be a hero in China
With my tenor belching tunes,
Burping with satisfaction,
Just as I'd do in Japan,
Where I would voraciously slurp
A homemade miso soup.

Not to mention
All those religious rules
That command you
To avoid the forbidden fruit,
And the best way
To get into heaven with Jesus.

Then, there's the old,
Watching after the youth.
In case their offspring don't follow
The old generation's creed,
Or the parents' unrealized dreams,
They become rascals to be redeemed.

Luckily, rules are just rules
That are audaciously broken
By resolute champs of freedom.
They are the true heroes,
Who without harming anyone,
Bring progress to all.

So Many Rules

Rules are just rules.
Who cares if they call me bizarre,
Even if they make fun of me.
All I care about is to be free.
How I define wild to me,
Running up and down
In my unpredictable life.

Make your own rules!
Live your life!

A Special Week

Another week unfolds.
I am ready to live it up
One day after the other
With plenty of hope,
From Sunday to Saturday,
Giving the very best of me,
But counting the days
Until Friday would come.

Monday is a manic day
When one feels confused.
There are no doubts,
You didn't sign up for this,
Unless you're a crazy hamster
Spinning the wheel of business.
Quick, give me the biggest mug,
Fill it up with extra-strong coffee.

When I was in my twenties,
I started a radical movement
To make Mondays illegal,
But sadly, the party broke up,
Because some members disagreed.
They wanted to ban Tuesdays as well,
They pushed even for Wednesdays,
Then Thursdays . . . too much!

The Tuscan Who Sold His Fiat to the Pope

Unnoticed comes baby Tuesday,
The first born of moody Monday,
Afflicted by its lack of personality.
But, it's not so bad, after all,
There's a margherita happy hour
After work at the Mexican cantina,
Suddenly, making Tuesdays feel better.

Wednesday boy follows,
This time with more character,
A hump day with funky bumps.
Not far, in the midst of the week,
Easygoing Thursday is coming.
I got something in my stomach.
For your safety, give me some space
To throw up before I throw back.

I see Friday eve's shooting star.
It's finally that time to let go.
The rat race will soon be ending.
I am so happy it's almost Friday.
My gosh, it sounds so sweet,
Seeing the shores in the distance
After riding the high tide of the week.
It's Thursday, and the fever is up!

Then . . . it's sunrise!
Let me repeat,
To everyone on board: It's sunrise!
Yes, you made it.
I want to jump, laugh, and scream.
It's Friday.
Who is going to drive you home tonight?
We haven't figured this out, but we will.

A Special Week

I have been waiting for you
Since Monday crossed over,
Its first child, Tuesday, was born, and
Hopeful Wednesday woke up.
On Thursday,
I sent smoke signals to the spirits.
Then, as sharp as a music note, you came,
Making me scream aloud:
THANK GOD FRIDAY IS HERE!

Good morning, Saturday.
That went fast.
What happens in "Fridayland" stays in "Fridayland."
Good night, bars and strippers.
I cannot believe how much of my weekly pay
Went to vodka and wine cellars.
Give me a few hours to recover
Before I give this divine day
My undivided attention,
Making it the most fun.

Let me introduce the last day of the week:
Sexy Sunday, and sex I shall have
Until my passion for you
Has cooked the pasta *al dente,*
And exhausted I'll go to sleep.
This doesn't mean that from Monday
Until Saturday there's no sex.
It just means that on Sunday
It's more and maybe twice as much!

Now that the week is over,
Let's do a recap:
Monday, the maniac child,
Tuesday, the boring child,
Wednesday, the hump with funky bumps,

The Tuscan Who Sold His Fiat to the Pope

Thursday, the day I throw up instead of throw back,
Friday, thank you, God, for you know what,
Saturday, I am crazy for you; touch me and you will know,
Sunday, make some pasta, sleep in,
enjoy, don't look ahead . . .

And when that Monday comes,
You will be all right,
Another Friday will be there soon,
Que sera, sera,
This has been a special week,
Just like the one that came before,
And the one that has yet to come.

A Bathroom Experience

If you travel to Europe
And need to go to the toilet,
Running fast in the hotel hallway,
You will soon discover
That you have few options,
Especially if you go number two,
Another way to say one has to poop.

Cleaning your rear bottom,
Also known as your precious ass,
Can be done with hygienic paper,
Not always as soft as you wish
But better than ficus leaves,
Or you can use another tool
Invented by a smart French dude.

The name of the fixture is "bidet."
Usually found right next to the bowl,
It looks like a lowered sink with a faucet,
To help regulate the water heat.
As you don't want to think,
Not even for a millisecond,
Of burning the finest of your regions.

I have no trouble explaining to you
How effective this tool is,

The Tuscan Who Sold His Fiat to the Pope

Which if properly operated,
Will give you an instant feeling
Of pleasure and cleanliness,
Making your ass completely free
From any uncomfortable tickling.

Your butt will be quite happy
To immerse itself in the warm running water,
And get rid of annoying residual pits,
Being restored with organic soap,
To the purity of Adam and Eve,
Just as they came out of the creation
From the depths of Earth's womb.

There's no need to rush,
Take your time with this ritual,
Play with the water and splash,
Let your intimate parts relax,
Sing a song if you wish,
Because this is time well spent,
Taking care of your body,
Meditating with your balls in your hands.

When you are done and ready
To go back to the business of this world,
You will see on the side of the bidet,
A little towel to dry yourself.
Make sure it's nice and neat,
Use it gently to caress your skin
And place it in the basket to be cleaned.

Before you leave the restroom,
Make sure to wash your hands.
Now you're ready to rejoin
The crap of this world,
Different but also similar

A Bathroom Experience

To the one you just left,
Although now you've got a smile on your face,
You feel relaxed and so much better.

Oh, thank you, inventor of the bidet,
I have no words for what you did.
You created one of the most gratifying fixtures,
And gave the proper attention
To the parts of the body
That at times are scorned
For no other reason
Than for being the expeller of what we eat.

(And why wouldn't you spend more time
To rethink what you eat,
After observing how bad you shit!)

Finally, I would like to conclude,
With a spontaneous plea of pride,
For our balls and asses
That are always neglected in our talks,
Like they had to be hidden,
Or be ashamed,
As if they were a disgrace.

Are you going number one?
Are you taking a piss?
Are you going number two?
Are you dumping some shit?

Come on, what's the big deal?
It's part of human nature,
It's time to let it go and embrace with joy,
The pleasure of sitting on the toilet,
The use (or rather abuse) of that bidet.

The Tuscan Who Sold His Fiat to the Pope

Live it up, my dear friend,
And get yourself clean!
Never worry for a second
About the envious constipated people!
Live free, and be spontaneous.
After all, it only matters
If you give a shit, and frankly,
Why would you,
even for a second?

P Zone

If you want to live well,
Stay young and sharp in the head;
The key thing to keep in mind
Is to stay cool in the P Zone.

What is that? Maybe a new diet?
It could be, to some extent
But rather than a diet,
It's freedom from any strains.

The P Zone is easy to follow,
As it only requires good usage
Of your P to get some P,
Stay active and motivated.

The worst thing you can do
Is to neglect the need of the P,
Because that will get you off,
Out of the zone, tense and stressed.

If you are a man, you will know:
She will get upset and annoyed;
It's your duty to get right back
In the P Zone, sooner than later.

The magical power of the P Zone
Is what you were designed for.

The Tuscan Who Sold His Fiat to the Pope

It's the best gift you ever got.
It's Mother Nature at her best.

You can't allow yourself to screw up.
You've got to stay focused.
It's the only game in town.
It's the P Zone you must trust.

Next time, instead of wasteful whining,
Make a quick assessment
And check where you are.
Take prompt action
And get right back in the
P Zone.

If you haven't figured it out,
Well, then . . .
Really?
What do women have
That starts with P
And rules the world?
While keeping your P
Securely under her spell,
And making you do all kinds of things?
Because for P,
A real man
Would give it all!

Believe me:
Follow this simple idea.
It's not a rule, rather a suggestion:
You cannot go wrong
If you stay focused
in the P Zone.
Yes!
It's

All
About
The
P.
What
Else?

Afterword, or Better Yet, Intermezzo

I first titled this chapter "Conclusion." Then I changed my mind. Why? Because I realized that there's no such thing as a conclusion. At most, it's an intermezzo between one act and another.

That is what I want to convey in this epic across cultures and imagination. Is it a final remark? No, absolutely not. Time and space make me wonder. If there is a wall at the end of the universe, what's behind that wall? And what's before the Big Bang? We belong to the circle of life: we are made of the same dust of the stars, and everything in the universe is at best, recycled matter that is altered from one state to the other.

In our society, we're in constant search of heroes. We don't realize that we are *all* heroes. It's *Eros* (the Greek word for "passion" and "love") that reclaims her role in the world, to express the infinite possibilities and combinations of the universe. Unfortunately, we suppress our Eros because we're afraid of her; afraid to let her shine a light—our light. We're afraid of rejection, or of being what we really are.

When I decided to publish this book, I had five minutes of hesitation. I thought, *Why does the world need another book? Why add another title to the thousands of books published daily in the United States? What is my book going to add to what has already been said by luminaries including Socrates, Epicurus, and Shakespeare?* But I was quick to shift the course of my thinking. It wasn't about putting some ink on paper to please an audience. This was about experiencing my Eros, exploring and expressing my passion. I am a part of the puzzle, just like everyone else.

It's for this reason that I left my "home" and ventured into this journey of heroes—aware that just as the many before and after me, I had a duty to share my experiences and life lessons.

I went to bed with this idea, and I had a dream. I was the water coming down the riverbank. On the way, I found sand, mud, and gravel and was jumping from one rocky section to the other, bypassing obstructing tree logs as I overflowed around the surrounding landscaping. There was no suffering. I enjoyed the journey all the way to the delta, where I began slowing down. I had to stop to look at the mesmerizing sight. In front of me was the ocean, an immeasurable body of my own matter, divinely stretched, reflecting the light of the sunset where I merged with the elements.

Passion for life is like the water of the river. It does not perceive the rocks and the tree logs as problems, but rather as opportunities to observe and navigate while continuing the journey toward its true purpose, which is to merge with the ocean. In fact, fighting the "obstacles" of life is the root of all suffering of the mind and the body. It begins in our mind. As Lucretius said two thousand years ago: "For as children tremble and fear everything in the blind darkness, so we in the light sometimes fear what is no more to be feared than the things children in the dark hold in terror and imagine will come true."

Resistance can take many forms, including accelerating the rhythm of life and seeing success as personal glorification rather than social contribution. We are not part of a competitive race with the rest of the world, but of the flow of the river of life. Ultimately, life's purpose is to merge with the ocean that transcends the giving and the receiving altogether.

As Michelangelo said, beauty is there at all times, and the task of the chisel is to remove the figure hiding inside the block of marble to bring it to light. This is my task with this book: to bring a smile to your face and mine, to interpret life as a moment to cheer, and to take things seriously but not too seriously.

I hope that all of you find your passion if you're still in search of it. Each one of us is called upon to be our own hero. I know for sure that with this book I have made my contribution and have kept my passion alive. However, I'm not done. I have more to say, in a unique way, which is my way. And, if any part of this book made you smile even for a second, then it makes my work that much more special, for which I thank you.

Love . . . and do what you will.

Written with passion by your companion in the journey of life.

Blessings.

Your Tuscan Friend with Lots of Humor

Acknowledgments

*W*riting has been an essential part of my life. You may call it love or even passion. From an early age, I learned to express my innermost thoughts through poems and short stories. The aspect of sharing my ideas is secondary. Rather, I observe the people and circumstances searching for meaning, as well as to connect with them.

I would like to thank my parents, Ada and Giovanni, for allowing me the freedom to travel and be independent at a young age, which I consider a priceless experience. They've always given me a sense of belonging—not only to family, but to my home country of Italy and to the world. I would like to acknowledge my grandmother, Bruna, who lived with our family until she passed away. She would often tell me stories about her life and the harsh postwar conditions of her childhood. I remember her fondly, and I miss her smile and enthusiasm for life. I want to thank my siblings, Gianna, Sara, Filippo, and Leonardo, for their affection and for keeping my childhood interesting. I would also like to credit my brother-in-law, Giovanni, for the cover and chapter illustrations.

I wouldn't be able to clearly convey my thoughts in English without the guidance of my daughter, Sharon. She's a beautiful presence in my life, and it was a gift to raise her and see her blossom. Thank you, Sharon, for all your support and for your help in editing this book. I'm also grateful for my son, William. He is strong, intelligent, quick-witted, and reminds me of myself as a young man. Being a parent has been one of the most rewarding experiences I've ever had.

I want to thank my partner, Viktoria. She is the love of my life—my muse, my confidante, my friend, and my companion in every new discovery I have—whether it's traveling the world or writing. This is how love works; it brings out the best in a person. I love you, Viktoria.

Thank you to all those who have crossed my path and changed my life for the better, including my friends, Sally and Maria.

I would like to thank my publisher, SkillBites, and particularly Judy Weintraub, CEO of SkillBites, who was vital to the publication of this book.

My native home of Florence was an influential factor throughout this process of discovery. Tuscany is the cradle of Etruscan culture, the Renaissance, and numerous historical figures who have shaped my heritage. I would like to acknowledge Michelangelo Buonarroti, Poggio Bracciolini, Lorenzo de' Medici, Botticelli, Galileo Galilei, Curzio Malaparte, and Roberto Benigni.

About the Author

Samuele Bagnai was born in Florence, Italy. He attended middle school in Vatican City in Rome, where he was part of a select group of students who were Pope John Paul II's altar boys. He moved to the United States in 1997 but did not forget his heritage or Tuscan humor, which kept him positive at heart. Samuele lives with his girlfriend, Viktoria, in San Diego, California. When not traveling, he loves reading, road biking, hiking, listening to all kinds of music, and of course, eating good food.

Instagram: @love_takes_you_to
Email: lovetakesyouto@gmail.com
Website: www.lovetakesyouto.com

Made in the USA
San Bernardino, CA
30 April 2019